INDIAN SIGN
LANGUAGE

Chief Flying Hawk (Sioux) and William Tomkins.

INDIAN SIGN
LANGUAGE

by WILLIAM TOMKINS

Dover Publications, Inc.

NEW YORK

Published in Canada by General Publishing Company, Ltd.,
30 Lesmill Road, Don Mills, Toronto, Ontario.
Published in the United Kingdom by Constable and Company, Ltd.,
10 Orange Street, London WC 2.

This Dover edition, first published in 1969, is an unabridged
and corrected republication of the 1931 fifth edition of the work
originally published by the author in San Diego, California,
under the title *Universal Indian Sign Language of the Plains
Indians of North America.*

Standard Book Number: 486-22029-X

Library of Congress Catalog Card Number: 69-13654

Manufactured in the United States of America

DOVER PUBLICATIONS, INC.
180 Varick Street
New York, N. Y. 10014

An old Sioux Indian friend of mine once said to me, in Sign Language at parting—

"May the Great Mystery make sunrise in your Heart."

Cordially Yours

Wm Tomkins

September 28, 1929.

My Dear Tomkins:

I have your letter of recent date and was very glad to hear from you.

I assure you it was a pleasure to meet you and Mrs. Tomkins while you were in Washington.

I want to congratulate you upon the good work you are doing to perpetuate the Indian Sign Language. Your book on "Universal Indian Sign Language" should be of great service to the Boy Scouts and I know it will be greatly appreciated by all who would like to see the Indian Sign Language perpetuated.

With kindest regards, I am

Very truly yours,

CHARLES CURTIS.

William Tomkins,
2 Park Avenue,
New York, N. Y.

SMITHSONIAN INSTITUTE
BUREAU OF AMERICAN ETHNOLOGY
WASHINGTON

Dear Mr. Tomkins:

I have read your most interesting and instructive book, "Universal Indian Sign Language," and consider it to be easily the best work of a practical nature that has been written on this subject. I did not think you would be able to improve upon the old book, but you have managed to do so.

The value of this work as a practical working text for Scouts cannot be overestimated. I am particularly pleased with the way in which you have retained only signs of true Indian origin, while at the same time making them practicable for modern use.

The chapters on pictography and ideographic writing furnish corollary topics which add to the interest and widen the usefulness of the book.

I feel that through the Boy Scouts and similar organizations your book will perpetuate one of the most interesting and characteristic cultural contributions of the aboriginal American.

Sincerely yours,

M. W. STERLING, Chief.

C O N T E N T S

Wambali Wi Yuta, "Sign Talking Eagle," Adopted Son of the Sioux,
Otherwise William Tomkins.

Ceremony of Adoption of William Tomkins by the Sioux.

The author and "BLAZE" in 1890.

The author and some of his friends.

Sons of Dakotah.

INTRODUCTORY NOTES

When a boy, from 1884 to 1894, the author lived on the edge of the Sioux Indian Reservation in Dakota Territory, located at Fort Sully, Cheyenne Agency, Pierre, and surrounding sections. He worked on the cow range and associated continuously with Indians. He learned some of the Sioux language, and made a study of sign. Since then, for many years, the interest has continued, and all known authorities on sign have been studied, as well as continued investigations with Blackfoot, Cheyenne, Sioux, Arapahoe, and other Indians of recognized sign-talking ability.

Of later years this effort has been inspired by the fact that there does not exist today any publication in print that can readily be obtained, covering exclusively the so-called Universal Indian Sign Language of the Plains Indians of North America.

There is a sentiment connected with the Indian Sign Language that attaches to no other. It is probably the first American language. It is the first and only American universal language. It may be the first universal language produced by any people. It is a genuine Indian language of great antiquity. It has a beauty and imagery possessed by few, if any, other languages. It is the foremost gesture language that the world has ever produced.

The author has lectured on Indian problems to many audiences, and at all times the keenest interest was shown in sign language demonstrations, and he has been requested, hundreds of times, to make the record permanent, and to thereby preserve and perpetuate the original American language which otherwise is fast passing away. This is shown by the fact that in 1885 Lewis F. Hadley, at that time a foremost authority on sign, claimed that as a result of extensive investigation he had determined that there were over 110,000 sign-talking Indians in the United States. Today there is a very small percentage of this number, due to the inroads of modern education, and many of our Indians, with college and university training, can speak better English than they can talk sign. This language was not created by anybody living today. If it belongs to anybody it belongs to Americans, and it is for the purpose of having it carried on by the youth of the United States that this little volume is compiled.

Very few works on the Indian Sign Language have ever been published. The first of importance was by Major Stephen H. Long in 1823, and gave about 100 signs. It is long since out of print.

In 1880 and 1881 Lieut.-Col. Garrick Mallery, writing for the Bureau of American Ethnology of the Smithsonian Institute, produced two valuable works, entitled, "Gesture Signs and Signals of the North American Indians," and "Sign Language Among the North American Indians." These were partially illustrated and are now out of print.

The next, and by far the most authoritative, work on Indian Sign Language was by Captain Wm. Philo Clark, U. S. Army. He was with the army in the Indian country from 1875 to 1880, and made a deep study of sign, with the result that in 1880 he was detailed by his commanding general to devote his time exclusively to the production of a book on same. He worked steadily on its preparation until 1884, when he died. The work was published in 1885, a small edition, and is now out of print and extremely difficult to obtain. It was not illustrated. This being America's leading authority on Indian sign, and differentiating as to the true Indian and deaf and dumb codes, the author has consulted it extensively in checking against his personal knowledge and studies extending over many years.

In 1887, 1890 and 1893, three works on "Primary Gestures," "Sign Talk," and "Indian Sign Talk," were produced by Lewis F. Hadley, a missionary in the Indian Territory. The latter was the more important, and was produced in an edition of but 75 copies. Of these but few copies are known to exist. There is one in the Smithsonian Institute, one in the Library of Congress, one in the Metropolitan Library, New York, one owned by Ernest Thompson Seton, and one in the library of Prof. J. C. Elsom of the University of Wisconsin, and through the kindness of Prof. Elsom the author possesses a photostatic copy. Next to the work by Capt. Clark, this is the foremost contribution to the study of Indian Sign Language, particularly as it contains several hundred graphic illustrations.

In 1918, Ernest Thompson Seton, the noted author of animal stories, compiled a splendid work, 282 pages and about 1700 signs, profusely illustrated. The work was named "Sign Talk", and it does not pretend to adhere to Indian signs but includes many desirable signs of the deaf and dumb, and other sources, comprising a very fine work, of value to any library.

Owing to the idiomatic form of the language there are certain fundamental differences which must be remembered. Every interrogation is made either wholly or in part by the question sign. Instead of saying "Where are you going?" the signs would be, QUESTION, YOU, GOING. Instead of "What do you want?" the signs would be QUESTION, YOU, WANT. The sign for "question" covers the words WHAT,

WHERE, WHY and WHEN. It is made to attract attention, to ask, to inquire, to examine.

The old-time Indian never used the terms "Good morning," or "Good evening," but had his own forms of greeting. The Sioux vocal language uses the term "How Coula?" meaning "How do you do, my friend?" The modern educated Indian uses the terms of the white man: so we believe that in this age the use of the terms "Good morning" and "Good evening" should not be out of place in talking sign between Whites or Indians, particularly as these words exist in sign language and are generally understood.

In sign language it is not customary to ask "What is your name?" because it has a different way of asking this question, viz: "What are you called?" the signs for which are QUESTION, YOU, CALLED.

In speaking of the age of a person, or of past or future time, the general custom is to say, "So many winters."

For time of day, make sign for SUN, holding hand toward the point in the heavens where the sun is at the time indicated. To specify a certain length of time during the day, indicate space on sky over which the sun passes.

Time is reckoned by the Indians as follows:—Days, by nights or sleeps; months, by moons; and years, by winters.

Present time is expressed by Indians by the sign NOW, and also by the sign TO-DAY, while occasionally, for emphasis, both signs are used.

What is understood to be the first person singular, is indicated by pointing to one's-self. The plural WE is made by the signs ME and ALL. YOU, ALL, means YE; while HE, ALL means THEY.

Gender is shown by adding the signs MAN or WOMAN.

Past tense is shown by adding LONG TIME.

Such words or articles, as A, THE, AN, IT, etc., are not used in sign language.

The syntax or sentence construction is naturally elemental and simple.

One very wide difference between the Indian Sign Language and the signs used by deaf and dumb, is shown in the word THINK. The originators of the Indian signs thought that thinking or understanding was done with the heart, and made the sign "drawn from the heart". Deaf mutes place extended fingers of the right hand against the forehead, to give the same meaning.

The deaf use a great deal of facial contortion and grimace. The Indian seldom uses facial expression, but maintains a composed and dignified countenance, the signs being sufficient of themselves.

There have been various confusing tribal differences of gesture in regard to TIME, present, past and future, and we have therefore recorded the most logical. See TIME, LONG TIME, AFTER, BEFORE, BEHIND, FUTURE and PAST. For time of day make the sign for SUN, holding hand at point in sky where sun is supposed to be represented. Indians estimate days by SLEEPS, or NIGHTS, months by MOONS, and years by WINTERS. In reckoning the age of a person the custom is to say "so many WINTERS."

With the passage of time some gestures have changed, as can be readily seen by the following. Before the introduction of the coffee-mill among the Indians, coffee was represented as a grain, or, more elaborately, by describing the process of preparing and drinking the beverage. The little coffee-mill killed off these gestures at once, and the motion made, as though turning the crank of the mill to grind the parched berry, is today understood as meaning COFFEE by practically all the plains Indians.

While not generally thought of as such, it is nevertheless a fact, that there is one composite group of over twenty million citizens of the United States who use a won-derfully comprehensive sign language every day, in fact could not get along without it, and, furthermore, they must use it or be guilty of violation of law. I refer to the gestures made by the great army of automobile drivers to indicate "Right turn," "Left turn," "Stop," etc.

Clark says: "It is very difficult to describe the most simple movements of the hands in space, so that a person who had never seen the movements would, by following the descriptions, make the correct motions."

In order to offset the possibility of mistake in this regard, I have herein illustrated practically all of the principal or root signs, in a manner which it is hoped will be clear to all.

On account of the lucid explanation shown in the cuts, it has been found possible to make verbal description very brief, thereby preventing the confusion which results from lengthy details.

It should be remembered that this is in large measure a skeleton language, because synonyms in general are covered by the basic word. For instance, the word ABAN-DONED means DIVORCED, THROWN AWAY, DISPLACED, DESERTED, FOR-

SAKEN. The word ABUSE can, according to its connection, mean SCOLD, ILL-TREAT, UPBRAID, DEFAME, DETRACT. The word AFRAID can mean SHRINK FROM, COWARDLY, SUSPICION, TEMERITY, DREAD, NERVOUS, FEARFUL.

Some slight liberties in spelling have been taken by the author, in order to simplify pronunciation. For instance, the word representing lodge, the conventional tent home, correctly speaking should be spelled TIPI: whereas phonetically the pronunciation is TEEPEE. We have therefore used the latter spelling.

Sign language is so faithful to nature and so natural in its expression that it is not probable that it will ever die. It has a practical utility, and should not be looked upon merely as a repetition of motions to be memorized from a limited list, but as a cultivated art, founded upon principles which can be readily applied by travelers. Sign language may be used to advantage at a distance, which the eye can reach but not the ear, and still more frequently when silence or secrecy is desired.

The author's thanks are due to a number of people who have helped him with the sign language. One of the first of these was William Fielder, a noted interpreter at Cheyenne Agency, Dakota; to Muzza Humpa (Iron Moccasin), and Cawgee Tonka (Big Crow), two Sioux living near Fort Sully, Dakota, and in general to many other Indians with whom he was acquainted at Cheyenne Agency, Pierre, Fort Pierre, and many places on the Sioux Reservation from 1885 to 1894.

Mr. R. C. Block of San Diego, California, a well-educated Cheyenne Indian and a fine sign-talker, has checked my manuscripts and passed favorably upon them.

In particular I wish to thank Mr. J. L. Clark, a Blackfoot Indian sculptor now located at Glacier Park, Montana, and who with great patience and kindness has gone over the entire language with me. Mr. Clark has the misfortune to be deaf and dumb, and this has developed him greatly as a sign talker. He is America's foremost Indian sculptor, and carves bears and other wild animals from blocks of wood, true to life.

Every author of a work on sign language in the past 100 years has emphasized the importance of illustration of same, therefore, realizing this fact, I have given much time to an endeavor to secure a capable artist. I have been most fortunate in securing the services of Mr. A. J. Stover of San Diego, an artist of wide experience and ability, and graduate of the Cleveland Art School. To his earnest devotion to the work much credit for the book is due, and he certainly has my best thanks. All of the sketches were posed by the author.

I have held back one thought for conclusion, and it is this: The beauty of Sign talk depends upon the manner of making the gestures. Movements should not be angular or jerky, but should rather be rounded and sweeping in their rendition. It is inspiring, and a thing of beauty, to witness a sign conversation between two capable Indian sign talkers. They are living in many parts of our country and should be cultivated wherever found.

Every sign in this work is a true Indian sign. Nothing has been borrowed from the deaf or from other sources, the compiler having adhered strictly to Indian origins. This, of necessity, makes for a briefer book than would otherwise be possible, but a conscientious effort has been made to make the book exactly what it purports to be, viz: the Indian Sign Language.

It is the most earnest hope of the author that this little work will so kindle enthusiasm in the breasts of thousands of boys and girls throughout the world, that the future, through this medium, will develop millions of young people who will be able to talk sign language with as great facility, grace and beauty as it was ever presented by any Indian in past time. This is the hope of the founder of Scouting, Sir Robert Baden Powell, Chief Scout of the World, who recently wrote to the author as follows:

THE BOY SCOUTS ASSOCIATION
25, Buckingham Palace Road,
LONDON, S. W.

My Dear Mr. Tomkins:

Thank you so much for your very kind thought of me and for sending me a copy of your Sign Language book. I had already commended it to Scouts in other countries in the hope that Scouts all over the world will take up the idea and use it as a common medium for bringing them all together in closer comradeship.

If it helps to bring about greater world friendship and understanding and avoidance of war your research into the Indian way of communication will have been well worth while, and you will have done a great thing for the world.

I cordially wish you every success and with many thanks and all good wishes, Believe me, Yours truly, ROBERT BADEN POWELL.

This work is dedicated to my wife, Grace M. Tomkins, whose constant interest and kindness have made possible and a pleasure the studies and research of years, and jointly with her it is dedicated to the youth of the world, in the belief that through the study of this subject there may be developed in all countries a multitude of sign talkers as fluent, graceful and rapid as our Indians themselves, and, as Sir Robert hopes, to the general good of humanity. THE AUTHOR.

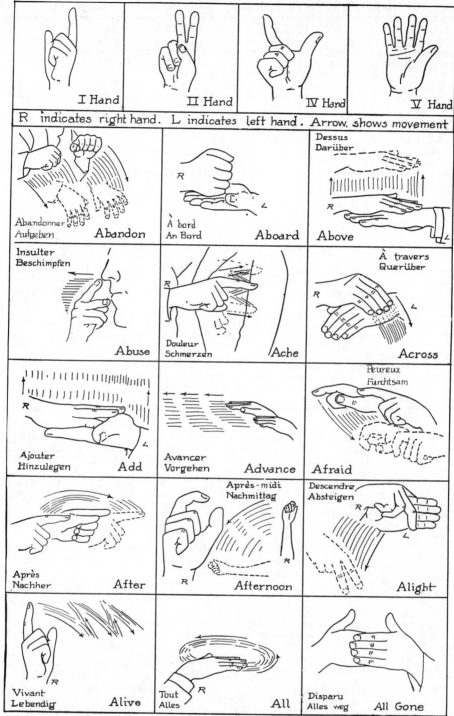

Line drawing shows beginning and dotted outline shows end of movement of hands.
Students must Compare Each Diagram with Explanation Found on Opposite Page.

A

ABANDON (meaning: throw away). With both closed hands held at left side near breast, drop them downwards and to rear, at same time opening them as though expelling some article.

ABOARD (meaning: sitting down on). Hold left hand flat, ten inches from body, palm up. Place right fist on left palm, with little finger down.

ABOVE (meaning one thing above another). Both hands backs up in front of body, the right resting on the left. Then raise the right more or less above the left.

ABSENT. Make signs for SIT and NO.

ABUSE (meaning: throwing lies against one). Bring right 2 hand in front of mouth; move the hand sharply outwards or towards person indicated; repeat.

ACCOMPANY. See WITH.

ACCOST. Make the sign for QUESTION.

ACCOST (meaning: to question). When party is at some distance hold right hand well up and wave to right and left two or three times.

ACHE (meaning: the darting sensations of pain). Push the right index finger over and parallel to the part afflicted; then make the sign for SICK.

ACROSS. The flat left hand, with back up, is held about twelve inches out from body. Then pass the partially compressed right hand over left on a curve.

ADD. Place right flat hand on palm of left in front of body, and lift them upwards several times in moves of about 3 inches, to indicate piling up.

ADVANCE. Point right flat hand forward, palm down, ten inches from body. Bring left hand in same position but between right hand and body. Then move both hands forward in slight jerks.

ADVANCE GUARD (The person in front). Left flat hand ten inches from center of body. Right 1 hand in front of left pointing upwards, then change to 2 hand, and move around to indicate LOOKING.

AFRAID (meaning: shrinks back from). Bring both 1 hands well out in front of breast; bring hands back a few inches and slightly downwards, while curving index fingers. Usually only right hand is used in making this sign.

AFRAID OF NO ONE. Point right index in several directions; then make signs for AFRAID and NO.

AFTER, (or FUTURE TIME.) Make sign for TIME, then advance the right 1 hand past and beyond the left hand.

AFTERNOON. Form an incomplete circle with thumb and index of right hand. Then raise toward a point directly overhead, and sweep down towards the horizon.

AGE. Indicate by showing number of winters. (See WINTER.)

AGENT (meaning: Indian Agent). Make signs for WHITE MAN, CHIEF, GIVE, and FOOD.

AGREEMENT. See TREATY.

AHEAD. Make the sign for BEFORE.

AID. Make signs for WORK and WITH.

AIM (meaning: "From the manner of using weapon"). If with rifle—aim accordingly; if with bow and arrow— bring hands up before breast with motion of drawing bow string.

AIRPLANE. Extend both arms straight out to each side, sway body imitating motion of plane; then swing hand in a curve from waist towards the sky. Then sign BIRD and EQUAL (a flexible modern sign, understood by Indians).

ALIGHT (to). Indicate whether from horse, wagon, etc. Then sweep 2 hand towards the ground.

ALIKE (meaning: that 2 people look alike). Make the signs for FACE and SAME.

ALIVE (meaning: walking about). Bring right 1 hand 10 inches from breast, then by wrist action make 3 zigzags.

ALL. Move right flat hand in horizontal circle from right to left, breast high.

ALL GONE. Point both extended hands at each other in front of breast. Then loosely wipe ends of fingers of right hand across palm and fingers of left, and vice versa.

ALLIANCE. Make sign for PEACE, and if for war purposes add signs GOING, WAR, WITH.

ALL RIGHT. Make sign for ALL and sign for GOOD.

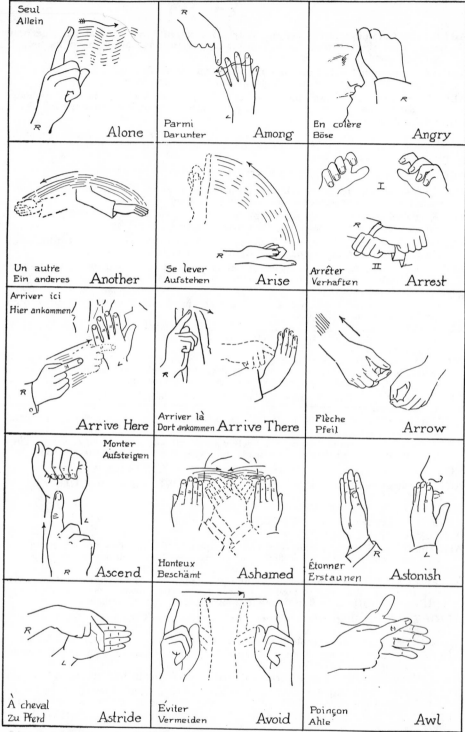

Seul
Allein
Alone

Parmi
Darunter
Among

En colère
Böse
Angry

Un autre
Ein anderes
Another

Se lever
Aufstehen
Arise

Arrêter
Verhaften
Arrest

Arriver ici
Hier ankommen
Arrive Here

Arriver là
Dort ankommen
Arrive There

Flèche
Pfeil
Arrow

Monter
Aufsteigen
Ascend

Honteux
Beschämt
Ashamed

Étonner
Erstaunen
Astonish

À cheval
Zu Pferd
Astride

Éviter
Vermeiden
Avoid

Poinçon
Ahle
Awl

Line drawing shows beginning and dotted outline shows end of movement of hands.
Students must Compare Each Diagram with Explanation Found on Opposite Page.

ALONE. Hold right 1 hand upwards in front of neck. Then move outwards in sinuous motion.

ALWAYS. Make the sign for FOREVER.

AMBITIOUS. Make sign for the person and sign for PUSH.

AMONG. Bring extended left 5 hand ten inches from breast, then weave right index through fingers of left.

ANCESTORS. Most Indians usually make sign for OLD PEOPLE. Some add LONG TIME.

AND. Make the sign for WITH.

ANGRY (meaning: mind twisted). Place closed right hand close to forehead, with back of thumb touching same; move hand slightly outwards and by wrist action give small twisting motion.

ANNIHILATE. See EXTERMINATE.

ANNOY (meaning: fluttering heart). Make the sign for HEART. Then flutter the 5 hand over the heart.

ANNUITIES. Make the sign for BLANKET, for FOOD and for DISTRIBUTE.

ANOTHER. Place compressed right hand over left breast, sweep hand upwards, outwards to right and downwards ending with back down.

ANTELOPE (meaning: pronged horns of animals). Hold both 4 hands beside head, palms forward.

APACHE—Indian (meaning: Elk horn fiddlers). Make the sign for Indian, then with right index rub the left index from end of finger to wrist and back again—2 or 3 times.

APPAREL. Pass both 4 hands over such position of body as is necessary to explain the clothing.

ARAPAHOE—Indian (meaning: MOTHER of all Tribes). First make sign for Indian, then with compressed right hand tap left breast two or three times, which is the MOTHER sign.

ARISE (meaning: to get up). Right 1 hand with back down, pointed to front, raise mostly by wrist action until back is outwards and index points upwards.

ARRANGE. Make signs for WORK and FIX.

ARREST (meaning: to seize hold of and tie at wrist). With both hands in front of body make as though seizing hold of a person. Then cross the wrists, hands closed.

ARRIVE HERE. Place flat left hand against left breast with back out. Hold right 1 hand one foot from body, then bring same briskly against back of left.

ARRIVE THERE. This is the reverse of previous sign. The left flat hand is held out in front; the right 1 hand held against breast, strikes out to palm of left.

ARROW (meaning: drawing an arrow from left hand). Near left breast, hold left cupped hand, then indicate drawing an arrow from same.

ARTILLERYMAN. Make sign for WHITE MAN, for SOLDIER, for WITH, and for CANNON.

ASCEND. Indicate in what way and what was ascended; for instance, a mountain, sign same with left hand, place right 1 hand with index on left wrist and gradually move same upward.

ASHAMED (meaning: drawing blanket over face). Both flat hands—opposite either cheek, backs outward. Cross right hand to left and left hand to right.

ASTONISH. Palm of left hand held over mouth. Many Indians also raise right hand. This gesture denotes great surprise, great pleasure, or great disappointment.

ASTRAY. Make the sign for HIDE.

ASTRIDE. Separate first and second fingers of right hand and set them astride of upright flat left hand.

ATTACK. Make sign for CHARGE.

ATTEMPT. Make the signs for WORK and PUSH.

ATTENTION. See QUESTION.

AUNT. Make signs for FATHER and SISTER, or MOTHER and SISTER.

AUTOMOBILE. Make the sign for WAGON and then imitate holding steering wheel. (Another modern sign understood by Indians.) A Cheyenne Indian used the signs WAGON, BY ITSELF, GO.

AUTUMN (meaning: falling leaf time). Make sign for TREE, for LEAF. Then let right hand pass slowly downwards to right with wavy motion.

AVOID. Hold 1 hands in front of shoulders pointing upwards. Pass right hand to left and left hand to right and have them miss in passing.

AWL. From manner of using same in sewing with sinew. Use right index as an awl and bore over left index.

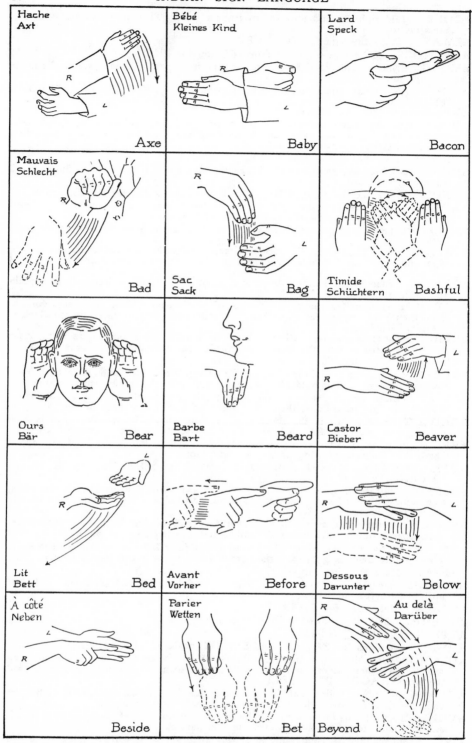

Hache
Axt

Axe

Bébé
Kleines Kind

Baby

Lard
Speck

Bacon

Mauvais
Schlecht

Bad

Sac
Sack

Bag

Timide
Schüchtern

Bashful

Ours
Bär   Bear

Barbe
Bart   Beard

Castor
Bieber   Beaver

Lit
Bett   Bed

Avant
Vorher   Before

Dessous
Darunter   Below

À côté
Neben

Beside

Parier
Wetten

Bet

Au delà
Darüber

Beyond

Line drawing shows beginning and dotted outline shows end of movement of hands.
Students must Compare Each Diagram with Explanation Found on Opposite Page.

AXE. Hold right elbow with left hand, extend right arm with hand held flat, and make as though chopping.

B

BABY. Place right closed hand across left wrist, palm side up, in position of holding a baby.

BACHELOR. Make the signs for MAN, MARRY and NO.

BACON. Bring extended left hand in front of breast pointing outwards; with right thumb and index clasp base of little finger and rub towards wrist and back again 2 or 3 times; then make the sign for EAT.

BAD (meaning: thrown away). Hold right fist near breast. Throw it out and down to right, and while doing so open the hand.

BAG. Hold left hand in form of opening of bag; then pass compressed right hand into opening. Finish by indicating sides of bag. Demonstrate a large bag by inside of circled arm.

BALD. Make the sign for HAIR. Touch top of head with flat hand. Then make sign WIPED OUT.

BARRACKS. Make the signs for WHITE SOLDIER and HOUSE.

BASHFUL. Make sign for ASHAMED.

BASIN (meaning: depression in the ground). With both 4 hands form a partial circle, then left hand holds position while compressed right hand scoops the ground.

BASKET. Make sign for KETTLE. Then interlock fingers to denote manner of construction.

BATTLE. Make sign for FIGHT, then sign for SHOOT, with both hands pointing towards each other.

BATTLESHIP. Make sign for BOAT, for FIRE, for BIG, and for BIG GUNS. (A flexible modern sign—understood by Indians.)

BAY. (Water). Make sign for WATER, then with right 4 hand out in front of body indicate form or shape of bay.

BAYONET. Make sign for GUN. Then place both 1 hands alongside one another, right index projecting beyond.

BE. Make the sign for SIT.

BEAR. The Crows and some other tribes hold partly closed hands alongside of head to indicate large ears—Others add to this a clawing motion with hands in front clawing downwards.

BEARD. For chin whiskers hang compressed hand below chin—for other kinds of whiskers place hands accordingly.

BEAUTIFUL. The preference seems to be to pass right flat hand downwards over face, then make sign for GOOD—some tribes hold up left hand and look into it as into a mirror.

BEAVER (meaning: tail of beaver striking mud or water). Hold left flat hand in front of body, right flat hand below same, then back of right hand strikes up against left palm sharply.

BED (meaning: spread blankets). Left hand, palm up, fingers extended pointing right front, close to left breast, right hand palm up, on same plane and close to left—move right hand well out in front and to right as though spreading blanket; add sign for SLEEP.

BEFORE, (or PAST TIME.) Point right and left 1 hands, to left, tandem, in position of TIME, then draw right hand towards the right and rear.

BEGIN. Make the sign for PUSH.

BEHIND. (Sense of time.) Make the sign for BEFORE, showing length of time by space between the hands.

BELOW. Both hands backs up in front of body, the left resting on the right; then drop the right more or less below the left to indicate desired distance.

BELT. Use the hands as though clasping on a belt.

BESIDE or BY. Make sign for WITH.

BET (meaning: to gamble). Inasmuch as the betting assumes card playing, the sign is made as though placing 2 stacks of money or chips.

BEYOND. Bring extended left hand, back up in front of body about ten inches, fingers pointing to right; bring extended right hand, back up, between left and body, same height, fingers pointing to left; swing the right hand outwards and upwards in curve beyond left hand, turning right hand back down in movement.

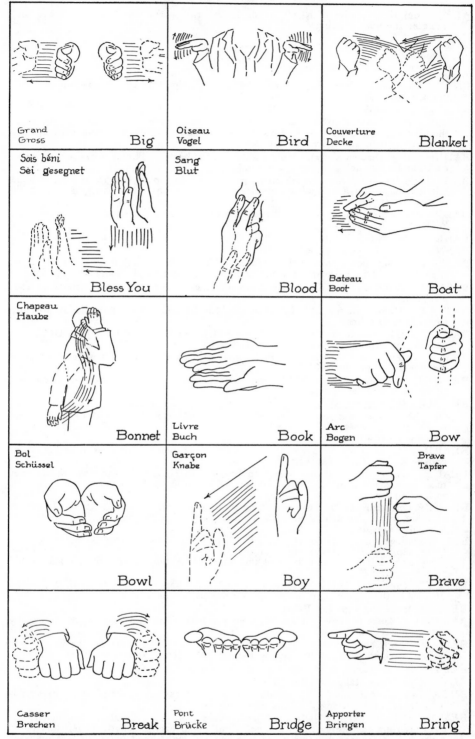

Grand
Gross   Big

Oiseau
Vogel   Bird

Couverture
Decke   Blanket

Sois béni
Sei gesegnet   Bless You

Sang
Blut   Blood

Bateau
Boot   Boat

Chapeau
Haube   Bonnet

Livre
Buch   Book

Arc
Bogen   Bow

Bol
Schüssel   Bowl

Garçon
Knabe   Boy

Brave
Tapfer   Brave

Casser
Brechen   Break

Pont
Brücke   Bridge

Apporter
Bringen   Bring

Line drawing shows beginning and dotted outline shows end of movement of hands.
Students must Compare Each Diagram with Explanation Found on Opposite Page.

BIBLE. Make the signs for BOOK, MEDICINE, and GREAT.

BICYCLE. A modern sign, like WAGON but with index fingers tandem, then add MAN, ABOARD, GO. Indians vary modern signs.

BIG. Bring compressed 5 hands in front of body, close together, palms in, fingers extended flat, upright, pointing to front, separate the hands—bringing them apart, but keeping them opposite each other.

BIRD (meaning: wings). With flat hands at shoulders, imitate motion of wings. Small birds rapidly, large birds slowly.

BITTER. Touch the tongue with tip of index of right hand and make the sign for BAD.

BLACK. The method most used by Indians is to point to something black. Have seen Indians simply use sign for COLOR as indicating BLACK; others make the sign for COLOR and touch hair or eyebrows.

BLACKFEET—Indians. Make sign for MOCCASIN and for BLACK.

BLANKET (meaning: wrapping about shoulders). Hold the closed hands at height of shoulders near neck, move the right hand to left, left to right, closing movement when wrists are crossed, right hand nearest body.

BLESS YOU. Raise both hands, palm outward, hands pointing front and upward, lower hands several inches, then push them slightly towards person.

BLIND. Place palmar surface of ends of fingers against closed eyes, then sign LOOK and NO.

BLOOD. Bring right hand in front of mouth, first and second fingers against nostrils, move hand downwards with tremulous motion.

BLUE. Make the sign for COLOR, then point to something blue in color, preferably the sky when clear.

BLUFF. Make the sign for MOUNTAIN, raising or lowering fist to indicate height.

BOAT. Hollowed hands held together indicate shape of boat, push out in front to show direction; for canoe make as though paddling; for row boat as though rowing; for steamboat add sign for FIRE.

BOIL (to). Make sign for WATER or FOOD; then sign for KETTLE and FIRE.

BONE. Make sign for the animal for DIE, LONG TIME. Touch part of body that produced bone, then point to something WHITE.

BONNET (war). Carry extended hands from front to rear alongside of head, then carry right hand from crown of head down to below body.

BOOK. Hold both hands in front of body, side by side, palms up, and look at them as if reading. Have seen Indians place palms together and open hands as though opening a book.

BORROW. Make the sign for GIVE (to you or to me) then BYANDBY or little while, and then GIVE—meaning, "Give to me a little while and I will give it back." They have no such word as loan.

BOW (meaning: bending bow to shoot). Left closed hand well out in front of body as though holding bow. Right closed hand held just back of same draws the bow string.

BOWL. Indicate shape with curved hands, held close together.

BOY. Make the sign for WHITE MAN or INDIAN, as the case may be, then bring right hand down on right side to height of boy, index finger pointing up.

BRAIN. Touch forehead with first 2 fingers of right hand.

BRAND. With index and thumb of right hand, form partial circle, other fingers closed —then press hand against left shoulder for shoulder brand, or against hip for hip brand.

BRAVE. Hold left fist 8 inches from center of body, bring right fist six inches above and a little in front of same. Strike downwards with right fist, by elbow action, second joints of right hand passing close to knuckles of left. Some Indians make the signs HEART and STRONG.

BREAD. Make sign for FLOUR. Then clap hands together as though making a cake, right hand on top; then reverse and repeat, left hand on top. The Indian method of making small fried bread.

BREAK (meaning: breaking a stick held horizontally in the closed hands). Hold closed hands together, backs up, then twist right to right, left to left, as though breaking a stick.

BREAKFAST. See EAT.

BRIDGE. Both flat hands, backs down, pointing to front, then make sign for RIVER and sign for ACROSS.

BRING. Move the right 1 hand well in front of body, index extended, then draw hand towards body, while curving index finger.

BROAD. Make the sign for BIG.

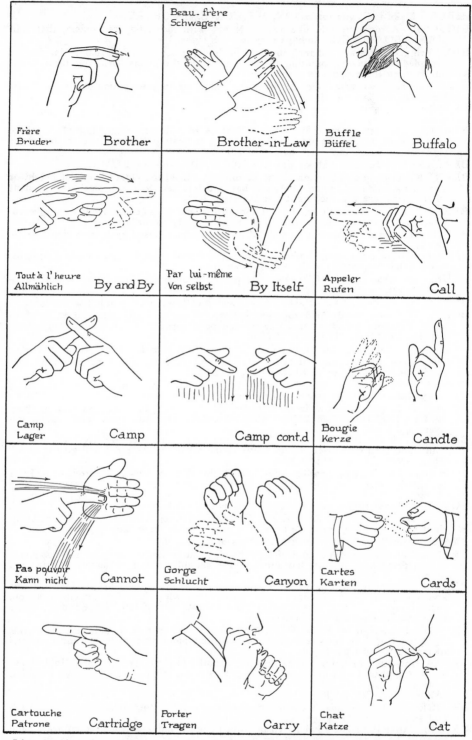

	Beau.-frère Schwager	
Frère Bruder Brother	Brother-in-Law	Buffle Büffel Buffalo
Tout à l' heure Allmählich By and By	Par lui-même Von selbst By Itself	Appeler Rufen Call
Camp Lager Camp	Camp cont.d	Bougie Kerze Candle
Pas pouvoir Kann nicht Cannot	Gorge Schlucht Canyon	Cartes Karten Cards
Cartouche Patrone Cartridge	Porter Tragen Carry	Chat Katze Cat

Line drawing shows beginning and dotted outline shows end of movement of hands.
Students must Compare Each Diagram with Explanation Found on Opposite Page.

BROTHER. Bring tips of extended and touching first and second fingers of right hand against lips, fingers horizontal, back up, carry hand straight out from mouth, then make sign for MAN.

BROTHER-IN-LAW. Cross arms on breasts, left arm inside, hands extended, then strike downwards in front with right hand.

BROOK. Make the signs for RIVER and SMALL.

BROWN. Make the sign for COLOR, then point to something BROWN.

BRUSH. Hold the hands as for GRASS, but with arms extended outward from the waist.

BUFFALO (meaning: horns of buffalo). Bring partly closed hands, palms inward, close to sides of head. Raise hands slightly until wrists are on edges of head, and carry slightly forward.

BUFFALO ROBE. Make sign for BUFFALO and for BLANKET.

BURN. Make the sign for FIRE. Then indicate what was burned or injured by the fire. If entirely consumed add WIPED OUT.

BURY. Make the signs for BLANKET, WRAP and DIG.

BUT. Make the sign for PERHAPS.

BUY. Make sign for MONEY and for EXCHANGE.

BY AND BY. Make the sign for FUTURE, advancing the right hand past and beyond the left hand. Some Indians make the sign for WAIT.

BY ITSELF. Hold extended right hand in front of right breast, with back down and fingers pointing to front; by wrist action strike the hand to left and towards body with a jerk, repeating two or three times. This is a metaphoric idiom used with other gestures. A gift with this sign becomes a "free gift." No gift expected in return. It also means FREEDOM, ALONE and SOLITARY.

C

CACHE. Make the sign for HIDE.

CALL OR CALLED. This is an important and much used sign. Use right hand with thumb touching index. Then snap out index finger as in word talk, but continue extending index. This is used for "Question you called"—meaning, "what are you called" or "what is your name."

CAMP. Make the sign for TEEPEE. Then with arms held about horizontal in front of body form with thumbs and indexes an incomplete circle, tips 1 inch apart. Lower the hands briskly few inches by elbow action.

CAMPFIRE. Make as though gathering something. Then make the signs for WOOD, FIRE, SIT and TALK.

CANDID. Make the sign for TRUE, for DAY and GOOD, indicating openness and clearness like the day, truth and goodness.

CANDLE. Hold left 1 hand in front of left shoulder, index pointing upwards. Make sign for FIRE with right hand pointed at left index and show length of candle on left arm.

CANDY. Make sign for SUGAR. Then hold left index vertically in front of body and with right hand indicate stripes on same.

CANNON (meaning: large gun). Make sign for GUN and for LARGE.

CANNOT (meaning: cannot go through, or bounced back). Hold left flat hand edgewise, well out in front of body. Point right index at center of left, then move right index forward until it strikes left palm, then bounces off and down to right.

CANOE. Make sign for BOAT, then with curved right hand held well out in front of body, indicate the curved bow of canoe.

CANYON (also GORGE, DEFILE, CHASM, GAP) (meaning: mountain, both sides). Hold both closed hands in front of face—several inches apart, then, still holding left hand in position, make as though to pass the right hand through the chasm.

CARDS. In nearly closed left hand make as though holding a deck of cards, then with right hand indicate dealing same to several players.

CARTRIDGE. Hold right 1 hand back nearly up, in front of body, index extended horizontally and pointing to front, thumb pressing against side of index, with tip just back of second joint indicating cartridge. Sometimes signs for GUN and SHOOT are also made.

CARRY. Place thumb side of right fist against right shoulder, then thumb side of left fist against right fist—in other words tandem—stoop slightly forward as though carrying a heavy bag or pack.

CAT (meaning: flat nose). With right thumb and index touching nose, tilt same slightly upwards, also indicate size of animal.

CATCH. Make the sign for TAKE.

CATTLE (meaning: spotted buffalo). Make signs for BUFFALO and SPOTTED.

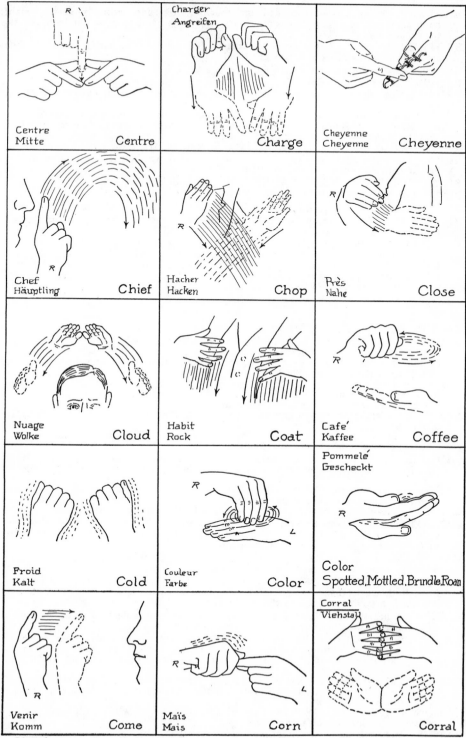

Centre Mitte **Centre**	Charger Angreifen **Charge**	Cheyenne Cheyenne **Cheyenne**
Chef Häuptling **Chief**	Hacher Hacken **Chop**	Près Nahe **Close**
Nuage Wolke **Cloud**	Habit Rock **Coat**	Cafe' Kaffee **Coffee**
Froid Kalt **Cold**	Couleur Farbe **Color**	Pommelé Gescheckt Color Spotted, Mottled, Brindle, Roan
Venir Komm **Come**	Maïs Mais **Corn**	Corral Viehstall **Corral**

Line drawing shows beginning and dotted outline shows end of movement of hands.
Students must Compare Each Diagram with Explanation Found on Opposite Page.

CAVALRYMAN. Make signs for WHITE MAN, SOLDIER and RIDE.

CENTRE. Make horizontal circle with index fingers and thumbs. Then holding left in same position place point of right index in circle just formed.

CERTAIN. Make the signs for I, KNOW and GOOD.

CHARGE (meaning: to charge against others). With backs up place closed hands near right shoulder, move hands sharply to front and left, at same time snapping them open.

CHARGE (meaning: charging against us). Reverse the above by holding fists well out in front and snapping hands open towards face.

CHEAT. Make signs for LYING and STEALING.

CHEYENNE—Indian (meaning: finger choppers). Make sign for INDIAN, then extend left index and with right index make as though to cut or slash same. A sign of mourning.

CHICKEN. Make sign for BIRD, sign for RED. Then place extended right hand on top of head, indicating comb.

CHIEF (meaning: elevated, rising above others and looking down at them). Hold right 1 hand at side pointing upwards, raise hand in gradual circle as high as top of head, then arch toward front and downward.

CHILD. Make the sign for MALE or FEMALE. Then hold compressed right hand upward at right side and drop to the height of the child.

CHIPPEWA—Indian. Make the signs for TREES and PEOPLE.

CHOP. Bring right flat hand near right breast, then by elbow action strike downwards to left, then reverse to left breast and strike downwards to right.

CHURCH. Make signs for GOD and HOUSE.

CIGAR. Make sign for TOBACCO. Then lay both indexes horizontally alongside of each and rotate one around the other (meaning: it's rolled).

CIGARETTE. Same as CIGAR but add LITTLE.

CITY. Make the sign for HOUSE and for MANY.

CLOSE (meaning: draw near). Slightly curved right hand well out in front of right shoulder, draw hand downwards and in towards body, holding hand flat and upright.

CLOUD. Hold extended hands horizontally, backs up, in front and higher than head, indexes touching; swing hands downwards in curve to each side, to signify dome of sky.

COAL. Make signs for HARD, FIRE, and GOOD.

COAT. Place spread hands on breasts then carry them down as though over garment.

COFFEE (meaning: grinding coffee in mill). Extend left hand, back down, in front of body; bring closed right hand few inches over left and move in small horizontal circle, as though turning a crank.

COLD. Both closed hands close to front of body, height of shoulder, body slightly bent. Give tremulous motion to hands and arms as though shivering from cold.

COLOR. Rub tips of right hand fingers in circle on back of left. Do not confuse this with the sign for Indian which is made by rubbing back of left hand with flat palmar surfaces of all the right hand fingers. A popular sign with all Indians when designating a color, is to look around, locate the color desired, and point to it.

COLOR (2) (spotted, mottled, brindle, roan). Rub the backs of the hands together. This represents any spotted or off color.

CONSIDER. See PERHAPS.

COMANCHE—Indian (meaning: snake). Make the sign for INDIAN and for SNAKE, pushing right 1 hand outwards with sinuous motion.

COME. Extend right 1 hand then sweep same toward face.

COMMENCE. Make the sign for PUSH.

COMPASS. Points of the compass are shown by the way an Indian records the sun. Thumb and index of right hand held across at left side indicates the sun rising in the east. In this manner the right side would indicate west, straight ahead would indicate south, and conversely would be north. A somewhat modern conception given by a leading Sioux authority.

CONCEAL. Make sign for HIDE.

CONGRESS. Make sign for BIG WHITE CHIEF'S HOUSE. Sign for BRING, from several directions, and sign for SITTING IN COUNCIL.

COOK. Make sign for MAKE (or WORK) and EAT (or FOOD).

CORN (meaning: shelling the corn). Project left index and thumb as though they were an ear of corn, then twist them with right index and thumb.

CORRAL. Make sign for TREE, lock fingers of right and left hands, then indicate circular enclosure by bringing them separately left and right in semi-circle.

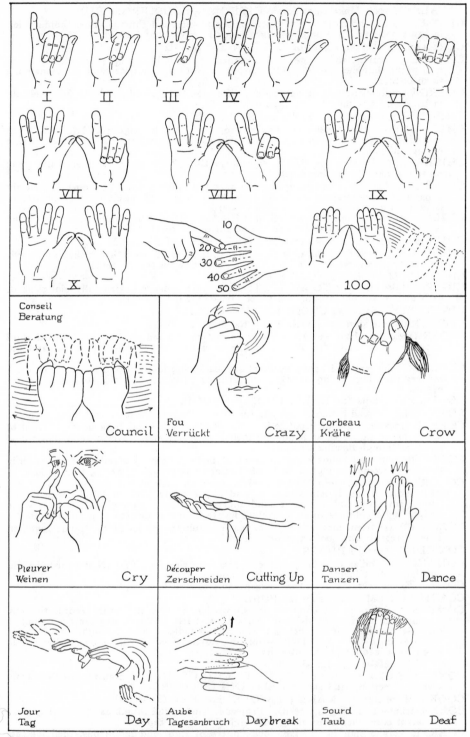

Line drawing shows beginning and dotted outline shows end of movement of hands.
Students must Compare Each Diagram with Explanation Found on Opposite Page.

COUNCIL (meaning: sitting in a circle and talking). Closed hands well out in front of body, little fingers touching, move hands in horizontal circle towards body to meet with backs to body—then add TALK to right and left.

COUNTING. The system of tens is universally used by our Indians in enumeration. In counting from one to ten, the usual way is to hold the closed right hand in front, the back towards and about height of shoulder, edges of hand pointing up; for one, the little finger is extended; two, the third; three, second; four, index; five, thumb; keeping fingers extended, separated, and pointing upwards; six, bring the closed left hand at same height, equally advanced, and near right, and extend the thumb; seven, extend left index; eight, second finger; nine, third finger; ten, little finger.

For twenty, open and close both hands twice.

Many tribes indicate a number of tens by first making the sign for ten, then hold extended left hand horizontally in front of body, and draw the tip of extended right index from base over the back of each finger to its tip, each motion of this kind representing ten and going as far as fifty; then holding the right hand in similar manner, mark the backs of its thumb and fingers with tip of left index to indicate from sixty to one hundred.

For counting hundreds hold up both 5 hands with both thumbs touching, hands held near right shoulder; then swing in a circle across to left and downwards.

A number of hundreds are counted on backs of hands same as in counting tens, first indicating that you are now dealing with hundreds.

COUNTRY. Make signs by pointing to the ground with right 1 hand; then spread both hands low to right and left.

COWARD. Point to or make sign for the person, and then make sign for AFRAID.

COYOTE. Make sign for WOLF and for SMALL.

CRAZY (meaning: brain in a whirl). Bring compressed right hand pointing upwards close to forehead. Turn the hand so as to make small horizontal circle, turning upwards to left with the sun. (To turn to right would mean MEDICINE).

CROSS (meaning: sulky). Make the signs HEART and BAD.

CROSS (meaning to cross a stream). Make the sign ACROSS.

CROW—Indian. Two signs have been used in this connection, for that in most general use sign BIRD and INDIAN. A less used sign as follows:—first make the sign for INDIAN, then hold fist above forehead, palm out, to indicate their manner of dressing the hair, i. e., pompadour.

CRY (meaning: tears). With both 1 hands at eyes indicate that tears are flowing by tracing their course down the face.

CUNNING. Make sign for WOLF.

CUTTING UP. With flat left hand, back upwards, held in front of left breast, use right flat hand as though to cut slice off palm of left, and repeat.

D

DAKOTA—Indians. (See SIOUX.)

DAM. Make sign for RIVER, and for HOLD.

DANCE (meaning: hopping action). Place both 5 hands in front of breast, pointing up, palms 6 inches apart; move up and down 3 inches, for 2 or 3 times.

DANGEROUS. With respect to a person, make the signs HEART and BAD. If. of a place, specify in what way it is dangerous.

DARK. Make sign for NIGHT and SAME; or hold extended hands in front of and close to eyes.

DAUGHTER. Make the sign for FEMALE, then with right compressed hand held upright indicate the height of girl.

DAY. Hold level flat hands, backs up, in front of face, and 4 inches apart; sweep hands up and out in a curve, ending opposite shoulders with palms up. For TODAY, first make sign NOW.

DAYBREAK. Place both extended hands, backs out, in same horizontal plane, right hand above with little finger touching left index; then raise the right hand a few inches.

DEAD. Make signs for DIE and SLEEP.

DEAF. Press palm of flat right hand against right ear; then make small circular motion with hand close to ear, and sign NO.

DECEIVE (meaning: he gives the lie). Make sign for GIVE and for LIE.

DEEP. To show depth of river or water, make sign for RIVER or WATER; then point downwards. If depth is slight, place hand on person to show how far the water rises on person or horse.

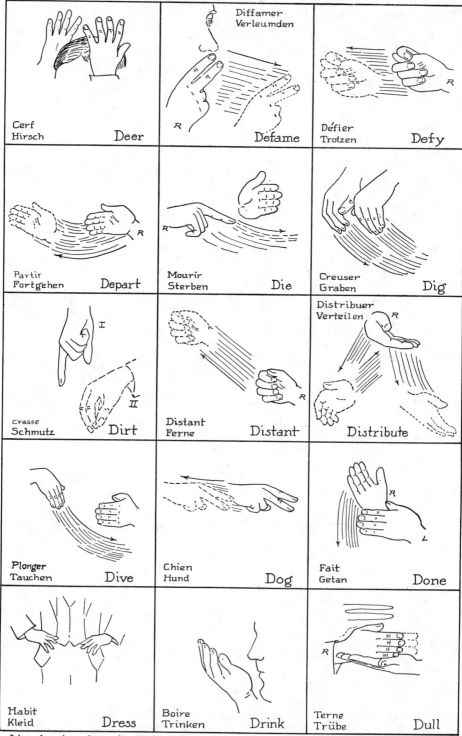

	Diffamer Verleumden	
Cerf Hirsch — Deer	Défame	Défier Trotzen — Defy
Partir Fortgehen — Depart	Mourir Sterben — Die	Creuser Graben — Dig
Crasse Schmutz — Dirt	Distant Ferne — Distant	Distribuer Verteilen — Distribute
Plonger Tauchen — Dive	Chien Hund — Dog	Fait Getan — Done
Habit Kleid — Dress	Boire Trinken — Drink	Terne Trübe — Dull

Line drawing shows beginning and dotted outline shows end of movement of hands. Students must Compare Each Diagram with Explanation Found on Opposite Page.

DEER. Indicate deer horns with both spread 5 hands held above sides of head.

DEFAME. Make the sign for ABUSE.

DEFY. Place thumb between index and second finger of right hand; push it sharply towards the person.

DEPART. Make sign for GO.

DESTROY. Make sign for EXTERMINATE.

DIE (meaning: going under). Hold the left flat hand, back out, well in front of body, fingers horizontal; bring right 1 hand on same plane and pointing to left hand, move right hand downwards and outwards.

DIG. Execute with both hands a pawing motion, moving hands from right front downwards, to left and rear on curve; repeating motion.

DINNER. See EAT.

DIRT. Point to ground with right index finger, then reach down and rub thumb and tips of fingers together.

DISGUST. Make the signs for HEART and TIRED. The head is sometimes turned to one side, and the idea conveyed by facial expression.

DISMOUNT. Make sign for HORSE; then raise right 2 hand and lower it, pointing fingers at ground.

DISTANT. Right hand, back to right, in front of right breast, a little lower than shoulder, hand partly closed and close to body; push the hand to front, raising it slightly. Very distant would be shown by extending arm to full length.

DISTRIBUTE (meaning: handing out). Bring right flat hand, back of same to right, well in front and a little to right of body; move hand slightly upwards to front, and then a little downwards; then take first position and make similar motion to left, as though giving to several persons.

DIVE. Hold left flat hand, back outwards, well in front of body, fingers pointing to right; hold right flat hand, back out, behind and little above left hand, fingers pointing downward; then move right hand down and out under left hand.

DIVORCE. Make the signs for HIS, WOMAN, and ABANDONED.

DO. Make the sign for WORK.

DO NOT. Make signs for WORK and NO.

DOCTOR. Make the signs for WHITE MAN, CHIEF and MEDICINE.

DOG (meaning: wolf drawing teepee poles). Draw right 2 hand across in front of body, from left to right.

DOLLAR. Make the sign for MONEY, and raise right index finger to indicate one.

DONE. Make the sign for END.

DOOR. Make the sign for TEEPEE or for HOUSE; hold left flat hand well in front of breast, back outwards and pointing to right; then place flat right hand on palm, and turn same over to right, as though little finger was a hinge.

DOUBT. Make the sign for PERHAPS.

DOWN. Point downwards with right index finger.

DREAM. Make signs for SLEEP, and SEE, and GOOD.

DRESS. Pass the spread thumb and index finger over that part of body represented as covered.

DRINK (meaning: drinking from the curved right hand). With fingers tight together partly compress the right hand as though to form a cup; carry to mouth from above downwards, as though drinking water.

DROUTH. Make signs for LONG TIME, RAIN, and NO.

DROWN. Make the sign for WATER; then sign whether LAKE or RIVER, and make sign for DIE.

DRUM. Place hands in first motion for KETTLE; then with left hand still in position, use partly closed right hand as drum-stick, and strike down several times.

DRUNKARD. Make sign for WHISKEY and sign for DRINK, repeating four or five times, and signs for MUCH and CRAZY.

DRY. To indicate that stream or spring is dry, make sign for STREAM (LITTLE RIVER), for WATER, and for ALL GONE.

DUCK. Make signs for BIRD and WATER, and gesture with right flat hand for flat hill.

DULL. Hold left flat hand in front of body, back down; then with lower edge of flat right hand saw back and forth 3 or 4 times; then make sign for BAD.

DUMB. Palm of right hand over mouth; then make the signs TALK and NO.

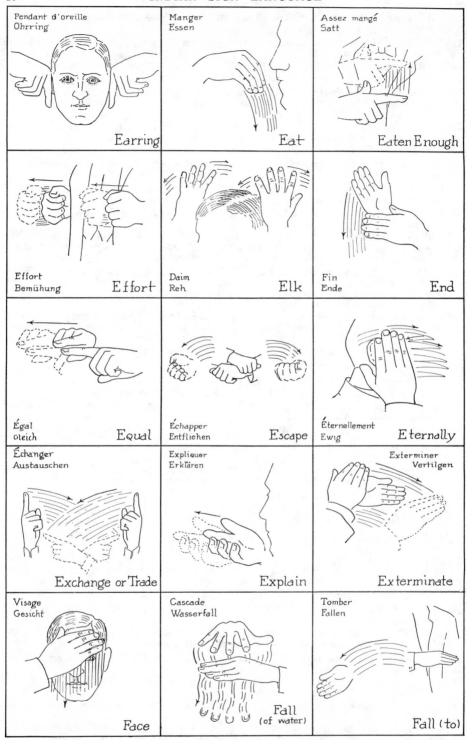

Pendant d'oreille
Ohrring
Earring

Manger
Essen
Eat

Assez mangé
Satt
Eaten Enough

Effort
Bemühung
Effort

Daim
Reh
Elk

Fin
Ende
End

Égal
Gleich
Equal

Échapper
Entfliehen
Escape

Éternellement
Ewig
Eternally

Échanger
Austauschen
Exchange or Trade

Expliquer
Erklären
Explain

Exterminer
Vertilgen
Exterminate

Visage
Gesicht
Face

Cascade
Wasserfall
Fall
(of water)

Tomber
Fallen
Fall (to)

Line drawing shows beginning and dotted outline shows end of movement of hands.
Students must Compare Each Diagram with Explanation Found on Opposite Page.

E

EAGLE (meaning: wings, and black tips of tail feathers). Make sign for BIRD; then hold horizontally the extended left flat hand, back up, in front of left breast, fingers pointing to front and right; then lay the lower edge of vertical extended right hand, back to right and outwards, fingers pointing to left and front, on back of left, on knuckles; move the right hand outwards and to right; then make sign for BLACK, representing the black end of the tail feathers. Occasionally the sign for TAIL is made.

EARLY. If early in the morning make signs for DAYBREAK, and LITTLE; if early in the evening, make signs for SUNSET, and LITTLE.

EARRING (meaning: long, narrow pendant). Point extended index fingers downward, other fingers and thumbs closed, alongside of ears, backs of hands towards head; shake hands a trifle, giving a trembling motion to index fingers.

EARTH. Point with right index to the ground, then reach down and rub thumb and tips of fingers together.

EAT. With nearly compressed right hand, pass tips of fingers in curve downward past mouth two or three times by wrist action.
Add location of sun in the sky to indicate breakfast, dinner or supper. (Modern).

EATEN ENOUGH (meaning: filled to the throat). Make the sign for EAT; then spread index and thumb of right hand close to breast; move the hand upwards to height of chin.

EFFORT. Make the sign for PUSH.

ELK (meaning: horns). With fingers extended and pointing upwards, place hands above head; move them to front and rear two or three times.

ELOPE. The Indian method of eloping is to STEAL the woman; so the proper signs are accordingly made, i.e., STEAL and WOMAN.

END (meaning: cut off). Hold left flat hand out in front of left breast, thumb upward; then with right flat hand strike down past finger tips of left hand.

ENEMY. Make the signs FRIEND and NO. Have seen Indians make the signs SHAKE HANDS and NO, though first sign is more general.

ENLIST. Make the signs for WORK and SOLDIER.

ENTER (meaning: to enter a TEEPEE, or stooping position in entering a lodge). Make sign for HOUSE; then hold compressed left hand well in front of body; bring partly compressed right hand downwards and outwards, under left.

EQUAL (meaning: even race). Hold 1 hands in front of breast, indexes two inches apart; move them both to front, keeping tips opposite, indicating an even race.

ESCAPE. With hands closed, cross the wrists; then separate hands quickly by swinging them to right and left and slightly upwards; then make the sign for GO.

ETERNALLY. Make the sign for FOREVER.

EVENING. With extended right hand, make the sign of SUN sinking in the west; then signs NIGHT, and LITTLE.

EXCHANGE or TRADE. Hold up 1 hands; then in semi-circle strike them past each other.

EXPLAIN. Hold extended right hand, back down, in front of, close to, and little lower than mouth, fingers pointing to left; by wrist action move hand outwards a few inches. To be spoken to or explained to, reverse the action, moving hand towards face.

EXTERMINATE (meaning: wiped out). Hold left flat hand in front of body; then wipe flat right hand across same.

F

FACE. Bring right flat hand down across front of face.

FAINT. Make the sign for DIE and for RECOVER.

FALL (Season). Make sign for AUTUMN.

FALL (of water). Make sign for RIVER; then hold flat hand, back out, in front of body; bring right hand, fingers slightly apart, over top of left hand and down with wavy motion.

FALL (to). Right flat hand in front of body, pointing to left, back up; swing hand in a curve, upwards and outwards, to right, then downwards while turning hand palm up.

FAME. The highest compliment you can pay an Indian is to say that he is a CHIEF, BRAVE; therefore make these signs to express fame.

FAR. Make the sign for DISTANT.

FARM. Make the sign for CORN and for WORK.

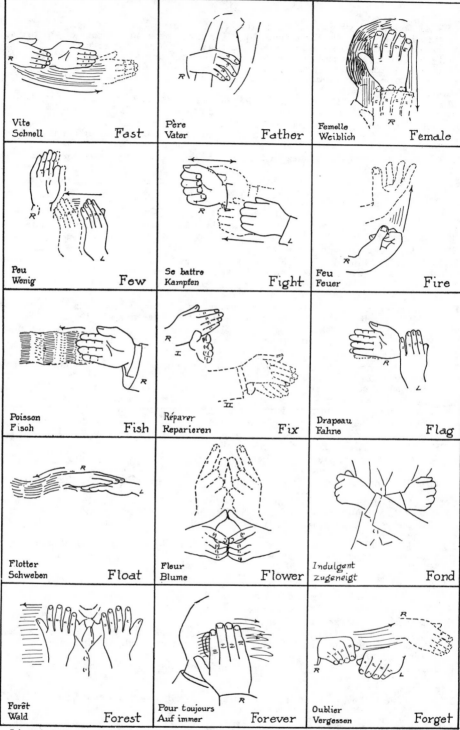

Vite Schnell **Fast**	Père Vater **Father**	Femelle Weiblich **Female**
Peu Wenig **Few**	Se battre Kampfen **Fight**	Feu Feuer **Fire**
Poisson Fisch **Fish**	Réparer Reparieren **Fix**	Drapeau Fahne **Flag**
Flotter Schweben **Float**	Fleur Blume **Flower**	Indulgent zugeneigt **Fond**
Forêt Wald **Forest**	Pour toujours Auf immer **Forever**	Oublier Vergessen **Forget**

Line drawing shows beginning and dotted outline shows end of movement of hands.
Students must Compare Each Diagram with Explanation Found on Opposite Page.

FAST (meaning: pass by). Hold left flat hand in front of body, back to left; then hold right flat hand, back to right, six inches to rear of left. Make right hand go swiftly past left in a curve very slightly downwards and then upwards.

FATHER. With compressed right hand gently tap right breast two or three times; then make the sign for MALE.

FATHER-IN-LAW. Make the sign for WIFE or HUSBAND, then FATHER.

FEAR. Make the sign for AFRAID.

FEAST. Make sign for WORK, for two or three kettles in a row, for BRING (from several directions); first part of sign for COUNCIL, and for EAT. (Repeat this latter two or three times).

FEATHER. For one feather worn as a decoration on the head, make sign for BIRD, for TAIL, and place extended index of right hand pointing up at back of head.

FEMALE (meaning: combing the hair). Place both hands on either side of head, fingers hooked; then stroke downwards as though combing the hair. Use of but right hand also correct.

FEW (meaning: compressed). Hold partly closed hands in front of body, palms towards each other, lower edges pointing to front, hands opposite, but heel of right hand height of index of left, and eight inches apart; move right hand to left, left to right until right is over left.

FIGHT. Bring loose fists, palms toward each other, in front of body, at height of shoulders, and three inches apart. Move right hand few inches towards body, while left goes outwards same distance; then reverse and repeat.

FINISHED. Make the sign for END.

FIRE (meaning: blaze). Carry right arm well down in front of body, fingers partially closed; raise hand slightly and snap fingers upwards. Repeat.

FIRE (meaning: discharge of weapon). See SHOOT.

FISH. Make sign for WATER, then hold flat right hand, back to right, at right of body near waist; then move the hand to front sinuously.

FIX. Hold left flat hand upwards, right flat hand crossing it at right angles; push edge of right across left, while left flattens with back up.

FLAG. Bring right flat hand out in front right shoulder; place fingers of left hand on wrist of right, then oscillate or wave right hand several times.

FLOAT. Indicate the WATER, RIVER, LAKE, etc. Bring extended left hand in front of breast, back up; lay right hand on it; then move hands with wavy motion to right.

FLOUR. Hold right hand, back to right, in front of body, and rub tips of fingers with tip of thumb; then point to something white and make sign for BREAD.

FLOWER. Make the sign for GRASS at waistline. Then make circle of thumb and index of both hands; then turn outside of hands under, until little fingers touch and thumbs and indexes point up. Some add SMELL and GOOD.

FLY. Make sign for WINGS, as in BIRD.

FOG. Make sign for WATER; then cross hands, fingers open, in front of eyes.

FOLLOW. With palms facing, left hand ahead, thrust both hands forward with zigzag motion.

FOND (meaning: pressed to the heart). Cross wrists, a little in front and above the heart, right nearest body, hands closed, backs out; press right forearm against body and left wrist against right. This expresses regard, liking, fondness, affection and love.

FOOD. Make the sign for EAT.

FOOL. Make the sign for CRAZY. (For UNWISE, INDISCREET or FOOLISH, add sign for LITTLE.)

FOOTPRINTS. Make sign for WALK and for SEE; fingers pointing to ground.

FOOTRACE. Make sign for RUN and for EQUAL. If one comes out ahead, move one finger to front.

FOREST. Hold open right and left hands ten inches out in front of shoulders, back outward, thumb and fingers spread. Move slightly upward, slowly, to indicate growth, then extend right hand to right and front indicating trees extend great distance, then add PLENTY.

FOREVER. Place the open right hand, palm towards right side of head, just clear of head; then move it forward and backward twice, past front and rear of head. In general use fifty years ago, according to Hadley.

FORGET (meaning: mental darkness). Almost make sign for NIGHT, by holding left hand steady in front and sweeping right hand around to left.

FORT (meaning: white soldier's house). Make the sign for WHITE, for SOLDIER, and for HOUSE.

FOUND. This is represented by I SAW IT. PICKED IT UP.

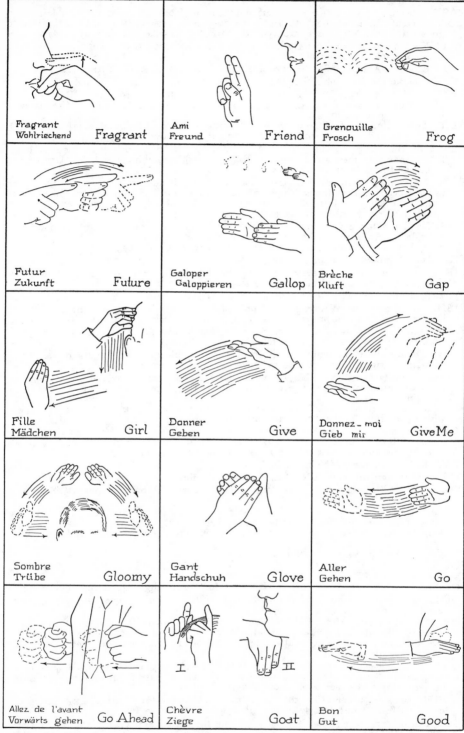

Fragrant
Wohlriechend   Fragrant

Ami
Freund   Friend

Grenouille
Frosch   Frog

Futur
Zukunft   Future

Galoper
Galoppieren   Gallop

Brèche
Kluft   Gap

Fille
Mädchen   Girl

Donner
Geben   Give

Donnez _ moi
Gieb mir   GiveMe

Sombre
Trübe   Gloomy

Gant
Handschuh   Glove

Aller
Gehen   Go

Allez de l'avant
Vorwärts gehen   Go Ahead

Chèvre
Ziege   Goat

Bon
Gut   Good

Line drawing shows beginning and dotted outline shows end of movement of hands.
Students must Compare Each Diagram with Explanation Found on Opposite Page.

FOX. Show size of animal and large, long tail with white tip.

FRAGRANT (meaning: smells good). Move the right 2 hand by wrist action upwards from chin, nose passing between tips of fingers; then sign GOOD.

FREEZE. Make the sign for COLD, for WATER, and for HARD.

FREEZE OVER (meaning: ice closing over a stream). Make sign for COLD and for WATER or RIVER; then hold flat hands, backs up, opposite shoulders, fingers pointing to front; move hands toward each other until index fingers touch. Representing ice formed on surface of water.

FRIEND (meaning: brothers growing up together). Hold right hand in front of neck, palm outwards, index and second fingers extending upwards; raise the hand until tips of fingers are high as head. Southern Indians make sign of shaking their own hands, which all Indians now understand.

FROG. Make sign for WATER; then compress right hand near right shoulder and make motion of frog jumping.

FUTURE. (Meaning—time in front.) Make the sign for TIME, then advance the right hand past and beyond the left hand.

G

GALLOP. Make sign for RIDE; then bring hands in front of center of body, hands held edgewise, left near the body, right in front of same; move the hands simultaneously up and down several times in vertical curves, to imitate action of horse.

GAP (meaning: mountain pass). With index and thumb spread, hold left hand out in front of breast, in form of gap; then pass right hand edgewise through the gap.

GENEROUS. Make signs for HEART and BIG.

GET. Make the sign for POSSESSION.

GIRL. Make the sign for WOMAN; then bring hand down on right side to indicate height; fingers compressed and pointing up.

GIVE. Hold right flat hand, back to right, pointing to front and upwards, in front of body at height of shoulder; move hand out and down.

GIVE ME. About height of neck, bring right well out in front of body, back of hand downwards and slightly to left, lower edge nearest to body, hand flat and pointing upwards; bring hand in towards body and lower slightly.

GIVE NAME TO. Make the signs for CALL and GIVE. Clark says: "A young man, after making his maiden effort on the war path, if he has met with success, 'sheds' his boyish name, and is given frequently the name by which some of the old men of his tribe have always been known."

GLAD (meaning: sunshine in the heart). Make sign for HEART; then sign for DAY or OPENING UP, and SUNRISE. Carrying hands into position on curves as indicated gives grace and beauty to movements.

GLOOMY (meaning: the clouds are close). Make the sign for CLOUDS; then draw them down to near the head.

GLOVE. Pass the spread thumb and index of right over left hand, meaning any covering for the hands.

GO. Hold flat right hand in front of body, back to right, pointing front and downwards; move hand to front, and by wrist action, raise fingers to front and upwards.

GO AHEAD. Make the sign for PUSH.

GOAT (meaning: horns, and whiskers under chin). Bring 1 hands alongside of head, pointing upwards, hands held just over ears; then place back of right wrist against under side of chin, hand compressed and pointing downward.

GOD (meaning: the great mystery). Make signs for MEDICINE and GREAT, and point to zenith.

GOLD. Make the sign for MONEY; then point to something YELLOW in color.

GONE. Make the signs for GO and LONG TIME.

GOOD (meaning: level with the heart). Hold the flat right hand, back up, in front of and close to left breast, pointing to left; move hand briskly well out to front and to right, keeping it in a horizontal plane.

GOOD EVENING. Make the signs for GOOD, DAY and SUNSET. (The true Indian version would be SUNSET, DAY and GOOD.)

GOOD MORNING. Make the signs for GOOD, DAY and SUNRISE. (To be exact, the Indian would say SUNRISE, DAY, and GOOD.)

GOOSE. Make slow sign for BIRD; then indicate triangular shape taken by flocks of geese in their migrations.

GRANDFATHER. Make the sign for FATHER, and for OLD, by rotating right hand by right ear to indicate that hearing was poor.

GRANDMOTHER. Make the sign for MOTHER, and for OLD, by rotating right hand by right ear to indicate that hearing was poor.

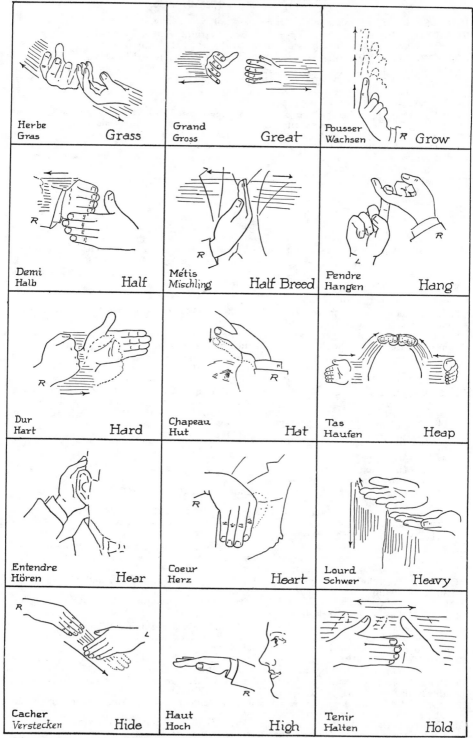

Herbe
Gras   Grass

Grand
Gross   Great

Pousser
Wachsen   Grow

Demi
Halb   Half

Métis
Mischling   Half Breed

Pendre
Hangen   Hang

Dur
Hart   Hard

Chapeau
Hut   Hat

Tas
Haufen   Heap

Entendre
Hören   Hear

Coeur
Herz   Heart

Lourd
Schwer   Heavy

Cacher
Verstecken   Hide

Haut
Hoch   High

Tenir
Halten   Hold

Line drawing shows beginning and dotted outline shows end of movement of hands.
Students must Compare Each Diagram with Explanation Found on Opposite Page.

GRASS. Hold the hands, back downwards, arms extended downwards to full length, in front of body, fingers extended, separated and slightly curved, pointing upwards; then swing hands apart.

GRAVE. Make signs for DIE and BURY.

GRAY (meaning: white and black). Make the signs for WHITE, LITTLE, BLACK, LITTLE, or make sign for COLOR and point to something gray.

GREAT. With palms toward each other bring extended hands out in front of breast; then separate the hands to right and left.

GREAT MYSTERY. Make the signs for MEDICINE and GREAT.

GREEN. Make the sign for COLOR; then point to the grass if convenient, otherwise to something green.

GRIEVE. Make sign for CRY, and for cutting off hair.

GROW. Hold right hand, back down, index extended, and pointing upwards, in front of body; hand held near the ground; raise hand by gentle jerks.

GUN. Make as though shooting gun, then add sign for FIRE. For rifle add working of lever.

H

HAIL. Make the sign for RAIN, for COLD; then indicate size of hailstones with curved index and thumb of right hand.

HAIR. To denote hair of human being, touch hair of head.

HALF. Hold flat left hand out in front of breast with back out; lay lower edge of right hand on upper edge of left, resting at knuckle of left index, back to right and front, fingers extending, touching; move right hand to right and outwards.

HALF BREED (meaning: half of body one kind, half of another). Place flat right hand upwards, in center of breast, little finger near breast; move hand one foot to left, then back and one foot to right. Have seen Sioux make the sign "One-half Indian, one-half white man."

HALT. Hold flat right hand palm outward, in front of body, height of shoulders; move hand sharply to front and downwards, stopping it suddenly. Some Indians raise the hand higher for emphasis.

HANDSOME. Make sign for BEAUTIFUL.

HANG (to) (meaning: as pendant). The left index is extended and held horizontally in front of body, other fingers closed, and the right index curved and hooked to it.

HAPPY. Make the sign for GLAD.

HARD. Hold out left hand palm, straight up; strike it with right fist two or three times.

HAT. Bring right hand, back outwards, in front close to and a little above head, index and thumb spread and nearly horizontal, other fingers closed; lower the hand until thumb and index are about opposite the eyes; spread thumb and index, passing down close to forehead, index to left, thumb to right.

HATCHET. Make signs for AXE and SMALL.

HAVE. Make the sign for POSSESSION.

HAWK. Make the sign for BIRD; then hold partially compressed right hand a little higher and in front of right shoulder; move swiftly to front and down with slight curve up, imitating a hawk's dive through the air after its prey.

HE or HIM. Point right index at person indicated.

HEADACHE. Make the sign for SICK, by imitating throbbing in front of head.

HEAP. First indicate gathering in from the sides, then bring hands upwards in curve to show the shape.

HEAR. Hold right cupped hand behind right ear.

HEART. Bring compressed right hand pointing downwards over heart.

HEAVEN. Point upwards with right index, looking up with reverence. (Modern.)

HEAVY. (meaning: cannot hold up). Hold out flat hands in front of body, palms up; raise hands slightly and let them drop a few inches.

HELP. Make the signs for WORK and WITH.

HER. Point right index at person indicated.

HERE. Make sign for SIT.

HIDE (to). Hold out left flat hand, pointing oblique to right; hold right hand in same relative position, pointing at left hand; then pass right down under left.

HIGH. Hold flat hand, back up, in front of right shoulder; then raise or lower to height desired to be shown.

HILL. Make the signs for MOUNTAIN and LITTLE.

HIS or HERS. Point to person and make sign for POSSESSION.

HOLD. Hold both hands, back out, with fingers spread; lay the fingers of one hand over the interstices of the other, as if to prevent anything passing through between the fingers; move the hands, held in this position, slightly to right and left, by elbow and shoulder action.

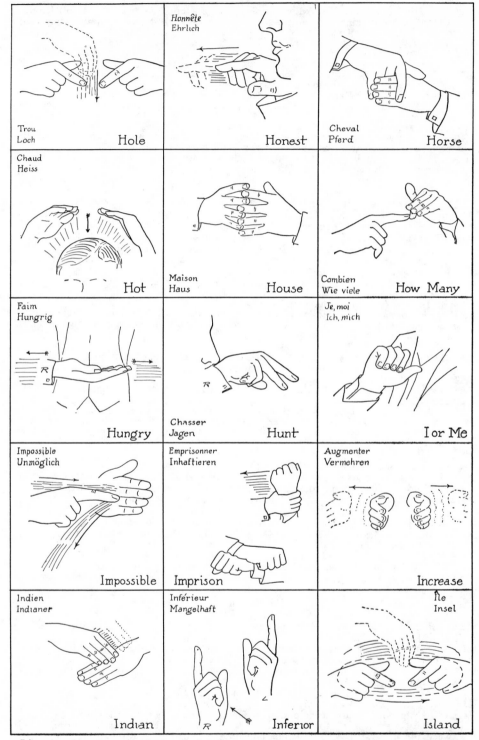

Trou
Loch   Hole

Honnête
Ehrlich   Honest

Cheval
Pferd   Horse

Chaud
Heiss   Hot

Maison
Haus   House

Combien
Wie viele   How Many

Faim
Hungrig   Hungry

Chasser
Jagen   Hunt

Je, moi
Ich, mich   I or Me

Impossible
Unmöglich   Impossible

Emprisonner
Inhaftieren   Imprison

Augmenter
Vermehren   Increase

Indien
Indianer   Indian

Inférieur
Mangelhaft   Inferior

Île
Insel   Island

Line drawing shows beginning and dotted outline shows end of movement of hands.
Students must Compare Each Diagram with Explanation Found on Opposite Page.

HOLE. Make circle with thumb and index of both hands; then, holding left in position, press compressed right through hole.

HOMELY. Pass palm of hand over face and make sign for BAD.

HONEST. Make the sign for TRUE.

HORSE. Hold left flat hand edgewise, back to left in front of left breast. Some Indians to make the sign more emphatic place the right index and second fingers astride the left hand.
The sign used in illustration is most generally used.

HORSERACE. Make sign for HORSE and for RACE.

HOSPITAL. Make signs for HOUSE, SICK, and MANY. Some Indians make signs for HOUSE and MEDICINE.

HOT (meaning: rays of sun pressing down). Hold flat hands above head, few inches apart; then bring hands down and slightly towards head.

HOUSE (meaning: corner of log house). With hands in front of body, interlace fingers near tips, fingers at right angles, horizontal. This is the primitive sign for house, though Cheyennes frequently indicate shape of gable roof with both 5 hands pointing up.

HOW MANY. Sign INTERROGATE or QUESTION; point left hand at 45 deg. angle to right and front; then with index of right hand strike little finger and others in succession. As fingers are struck they remain down.

HOW MUCH. Expressed by HOW MANY. How much money would be, how many dollars?

HUNDRED. See COUNTING.

HUNGRY (meaning: cuts one in two). Hold little finger edge of hand against center of body; then move to right and left as though cutting in two.

HUNT. Make sign for WOLF, that is bring 2 hand near eye and move it around.

HURRY. Make the signs for WORK, and FAST.

HUSBAND. Make the signs for MALE, and MARRY.

I

I (meaning: myself). With right extended thumb touch center of breast.

ICE. Make signs for WATER, for COLD, and bring hands together as in FREEZE OVER.

ICICLE. Make sign for WATER, for COLD, and hold right index in front of body, pointing downward.

IMPOSSIBLE. Make sign for CANNOT.

IMPRISON (meaning: seizing hold of). Hold left fist, back to left, a little higher and in front of left shoulder; then seize left wrist with right hand and pull it some inches to right; then cross wrists in front of body, right on top, hands closed.

IN. For a person "in my house," make signs for HOUSE and SIT.

INCREASE. Hold hands out in front of body, palms toward each other, few inches apart, fingers pointing to front; separate hands and move them out and apart by gentle jerks.

INDIAN. Hold the flat left hand, back up, in front, and rub it from wrist to knuckles, back and forth, twice.

INFANTRY. Make signs for WHITE, SOLDIERS and WALK.

INFERIOR (meaning: in rank or influence). Index fingers side by side, extended pointing upwards; one index to represent the inferior is held a little lower than the other. For several persons inferior to one, right index is held a little higher than the extended fingers of left.

INJURE (meaning: doing evil to). Referring to someone else, make signs for WORK and BAD. Referring to one's self, make the signs for DO, TO ME, BAD.

INTERPRETER. Make the signs for HE, TALKS, LITTLE, WHITE MAN, TALK and name particular language.

INTERROGATE. As this means QUESTION, the reader is referred to the explanation given under that head.

IRON. Make the sign for HARD and point to something metallic.

ISLAND. Form an incomplete circle with thumbs and indexes of both hands out in front of body, ends of thumbs and indexes an inch apart; leave left hand in position, and make sign for WATER with right hand; then with tips of compressed right hand draw a circle outside the circle first formed.

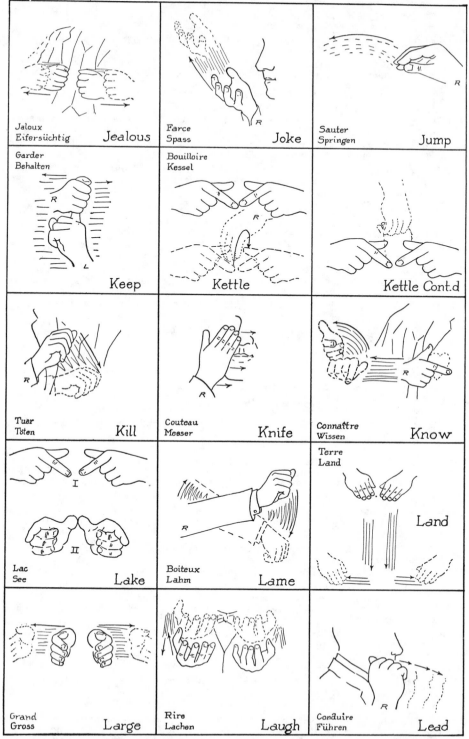

Jaloux
Eifersüchtig   Jealous

Farce
Spass   Joke

Sauter
Springen   Jump

Garder
Behalten   Keep

Bouilloire
Kessel   Kettle

Kettle Cont.d

Tuar
Töten   Kill

Couteau
Messer   Knife

Connaître
Wissen   Know

Lac
See   Lake

Boiteux
Lahm   Lame

Terre
Land   Land

Grand
Gross   Large

Rire
Lachen   Laugh

Conduire
Führen   Lead

Line drawing shows beginning and dotted outline shows end of movement of hands.
Students must Compare Each Diagram with Explanation Found on Opposite Page.

J

JEALOUS (meaning: elbowing to one side). Hold closed hands near right and left breasts; move right elbow a little to right and rear, then left elbow a little to left and rear. Repeat.

JOKE. Hold right hand with back down, in front of mouth, fingers separated, partly curved and pointing forward; move hand to front and upwards. This is a recognized Indian sign, but not in general use.

JOYOUS. Make signs for HEART and GLAD.

JUMP. Hold compressed right hand, with back to right, close to right shoulder, fingers pointing to front; move hand to front, upwards, over, and down in vertical curve.

JUNIOR. For persons or officers this is generally indicated as in INFERIOR. The tip of one index lower than the other, the distance determining the difference in rank.

K

KEEP. With right hand grasp left index firmly and move hands slightly to right and left.

KEEP CLOSE. Make the signs for GOOD and CLOSE.

KEEP QUIET. Make sign for HALT, and repeat; then by lowering the hand gently the meaning would be, "Fear not," "Do not be anxious," etc.

KETTLE. Form an incomplete circle as in ISLAND; then with left hand in position carry partially-closed right hand across and down over imaginary kettle, making motion as though about to lift it by the handle.

KILL. Bring right hand in front of right shoulder, hand nearly closed; strike to front downwards and a little to left, stopping hand suddenly with slight rebound.

KINSHIP (meaning: near or distant from one source). Bring tips of extended, touching, first and second fingers of right hand against lips, as in sign for BROTHER; then make the sign for CLOSE or DISTANT, as relationship may be.

KNIFE (meaning: cutting a piece of meat, held with the left hand and with teeth). Hold right flat hand close to face, lower edge just over mouth; move the hand upwards and to left two or three times, as if trying to cut with lower edge of hand. Sometimes left hand is held in front of and a little higher than right, as though holding meat.

KNOW. Hold right hand, back up, close to left breast; sweep hand outwards and slightly upwards, turning hand by wrist action until palm nearly up; thumb and index extended, other fingers closed, thumb and index horizontal, index pointing nearly to left, thumb pointing to front.

KNOW NOT. Make the sign for KNOW, then open hand and sweep it to the right, making the sign NO.

L

LAKE (meaning: water and shape). Make sign for WATER; then with thumbs and index fingers make an incomplete horizontal circle with space of one inch between tips; then swing wrists together, tips of indexes apart.

LAME (meaning: limping motion of animals). Hold closed right hand, palm down, one foot in front of right breast; move hand slightly to front, and by wrist action bend the hand downwards and to left, repeating motion.

LAND. Push both flat hands toward the ground, then spread them sideways.

LARGE. Make the sign for BIG, and if very big, add sign for HIGH.

LASSO. Make sign for ROPE; then make as though to swing and throw same forward; then draw the hand back quickly as though catching the animal.

LAST. Bring right and left indexes together well out to left of body, representing a race; then pull right hand away back, representing last in the race.

LAST YEAR. Make the signs for WINTER and BEYOND.

LAUGH. Hold both 5 hands partly closed, in front of both breasts, palms up; then move them up and down.

LAW. Make the sign for TRUE.

LEAD (to) (meaning: leading a pony with lariat). Hold closed right hand, back to right, in front, close to and a little higher than right shoulder; move the hand to front by gentle jerks.

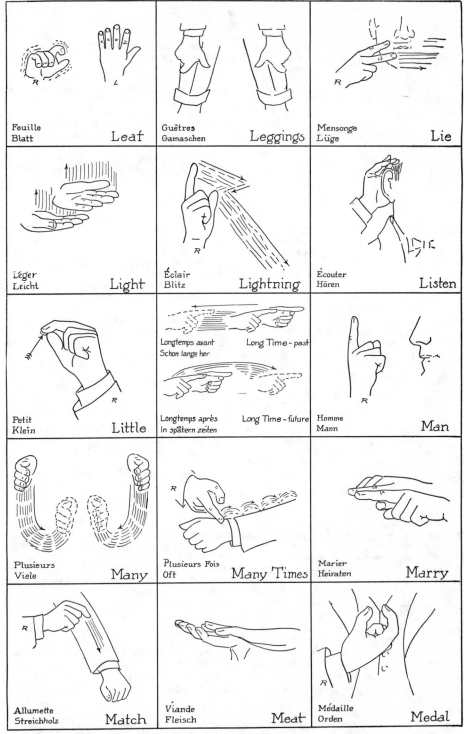

Feuille Blatt **Leaf**	Guêtres Gamaschen **Leggings**	Mensonge Lüge **Lie**
Léger Leicht **Light**	Éclair Blitz **Lightning**	Écouter Hören **Listen**
Petit Klein **Little**	Longtemps avant / Schon lange her — **Long Time – past** Longtemps après / In spätern zeiten — **Long Time – future**	Homme Mann **Man**
Plusieurs Viele **Many**	Plusieurs Fois Oft **Many Times**	Marier Heiraten **Marry**
Allumette Streichholz **Match**	Viande Fleisch **Meat**	Médaille Orden **Medal**

Line drawing shows beginning and dotted outline shows end of movement of hands.
Students must Compare Each Diagram with Explanation Found on Opposite Page.

LEAF. Make the sign for TREE; then hold right hand out in front of shoulder, index and thumb curved, one inch between tips, other fingers closed, back of hand nearly to right, lower edge pointing to front and upwards; give a wavy motion to hand to represent leaf on limb of tree.

LEGGINGS. Pass hands upwards over that portion of legs covered by leggings, thumb and index spread, backs of hands outwards.

LEND. See BORROW.

LIAR. Make sign for the person and for LIE.

LIBERATE. Make signs for HOLD and GO.

LIE (meaning: two tongues or forked tongue). Bring right 2 hand to right of mouth, fingers pointing to left; move the hand to left past mouth.

LIGHT (not heavy). Hold extended flat hands, back down, at same height in front of body, few inches apart, fingers pointing to front; raise hands briskly by wrist action.

LIGHT (not dark). Make the sign for DAY.

LIGHTNING (meaning: zigzag flash). Point right index upward; then move hand to right, rear and downwards in jerky motion, to imitate lightning flash.

LIKE. Make sign for EQUAL.

LISTEN. Hold right 4 hand, cupped near right ear; .turn hand slightly back and forth by wrist action.

LITTLE. Hold right hand at height of shoulder, back to right, end of thumb pressing against inner surface of index, so that only the end of index is seen beyond the thumb nail.

LITTLE TALK. See TALK.

LIVE. See ALIVE; also RECOVER.

LIVER. Place extended hands over location of liver, then give them a tremulous motion.

LODGE. See TEEPEE.

LONG TIME. Make the sign for TIME, then for PAST TIME continue drawing right hand towards the right while pushing left index slightly forward. For FUTURE TIME, hold left index in position and pass right index past and beyond the left.

LOOK. Make the sign for SEE.

LOST. Make sign for HIDE.

LOVE. Make the sign for FOND, with more intense pressure.

LOW. Hold right flat hand, back up, towards the ground at height desired.

LUNG. Hold right hand, fingers nearly extended and separated, over breast.

M

MAD. Make sign for ANGRY.

MAKE. Use sign for WORK.

MALE. Elevate the right index, back out, in front of face. Same as MAN.

MAN. Elevate the right index, back out, in front of face. Same as MALE.

MANY. Hold hands well in front, to right and left of body, fingers curved and pointing to front; move hands towards each other on vertical curve downwards; move them slightly upwards as though grasping hands, and finish full movement with hands opposite and few inches apart.

MANY TIMES (also, EVERY LITTLE WHILE). Hold left forearm horizontally in front of left breast, pointing front and right; touch forearm of left several times with side of tip of extended index of right hand, other fingers and thumb closed, back of hand nearly to front; commencing near left wrist and moving hand towards elbow. This is also used to mean: OFTEN, ALL THE TIME, and WHILE.

MARRY (meaning: trade or purchase). Make sign for TRADE; then join index fingers, side by side, pointing to front.

MARVELOUS. See MEDICINE.

MATCH (lucifer). With right hand hold match between thumb and index; then rub quickly against left forearm, as though scratching a match.

MATE or CHUM. Make the signs for FRIEND and EQUAL.

MAY-BE-SO. Same as PERHAPS.

ME. Point right thumb at breast.

MEAN (meaning: compressed heart). Make the signs for HEART and SMALL.

MEAT. Hold flat left hand, back up, in front of left breast; then with the flat right hand, palm up, slice imaginary pieces off the left palm.

MEDAL. Make an incomplete circle with thumb and index of right hand, spaced one inch between tips, other fingers closed, and place little finger on center of breast.

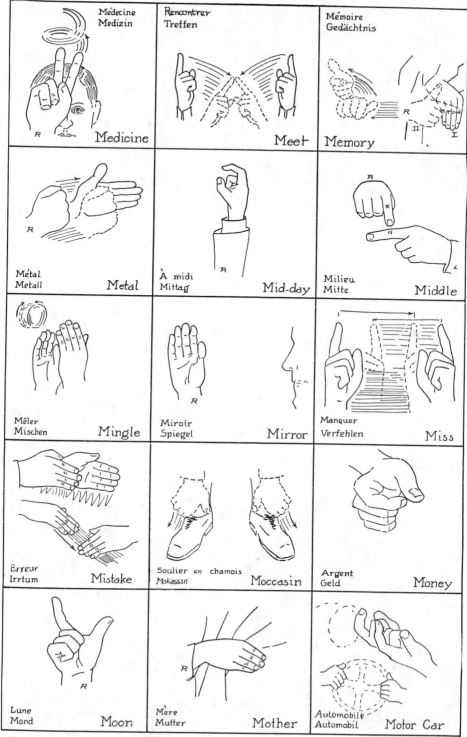

Médecine / Medizin — Medicine

Rencontrer / Treffen — Meet

Mémoire / Gedächtnis — Memory

Métal / Metall — Metal

À midi / Mittag — Mid-day

Milieu / Mitte — Middle

Mêler / Mischen — Mingle

Miroir / Spiegel — Mirror

Manquer / Verfehlen — Miss

Erreur / Irrtum — Mistake

Soulier en chamois / Mokassin — Moccasin

Argent / Geld — Money

Lune / Mond — Moon

Mère / Mutter — Mother

Automobile / Automobil — Motor Car

Line drawing shows beginning and dotted outline shows end of movement of hands.
Students must Compare Each Diagram with Explanation Found on Opposite Page.

MEDICINE (meaning: mysterious and unknown). Hold right 2 hand close to forehead, palm outwards; index and second fingers separated and pointing upwards, others and thumb closed; move hand upwards while turning from right to left in a spiral.

MEDICINE MAN. Make the sign for MAN and for MEDICINE.

MAKING BAD MEDICINE, or MAKING GOOD MEDICINE. Many Indians use this idiom, which is somewhat typical. To express either of the above, make signs accordingly.

MEET (to). Hold 1 hands opposite each other, pointing upwards; bring the hands towards each other until tips of index fingers touch.

MELANCHOLY. Make the signs for HEART and SICK.

MEMORY. Make the signs for HEART and KNOW.

METAL. There is no general sign for this except that for HARD. Anything made of metal must be pointed to or touched.

METEOR. Make sign for STAR, and with hand in that position make sign for FIRE; and then let it drop in a wavy, tremulous motion.

MID-DAY. Indicate that the sun is exactly overhead, or make the signs for DAY and MIDDLE.

MIDDLE. Hold left 1 hand well in front of left breast, with back to left; hold right 1 hand in front of right breast, raise it slightly up and over in small semicircle until tip of right index rests on middle joint of left index.

MIDNIGHT. Make the signs for NIGHT and MIDDLE.

MIDWINTER. Make the sign for WINTER and for MIDDLE.

MIGRATE (meaning: of birds). Make sign for BIRD, MANY and FLYING to south or north.

MILKY-WAY (meaning: ghosts, or dead men's road). Make sign for DIE, for TRAIL; then with right flat hand fully extended sweep in a segment of circle across that part of the sky.

MIND. Touch the two first fingers of right hand to forehead.

MINGLE. Hold slightly compressed hands out in front of body, opposite neck, hands pointing upward, close together, move them one about the other in circles, surfaces touching.

MIRROR. Hold up flat right hand with palm twelve inches from face, fingers pointing upwards. This represents a hand mirror.

MISLEAD. Make sign for TRAIL; then show deception by pushing right index out at a different angle.

MISS (to). Make the sign for AVOID.

MISTAKE. Make the signs for WORK and HIDE.

MIX. To mix by stirring imitate the motion. To mix otherwise, make the sign for MINGLE.

MOCCASIN. Pass spread thumbs and indexes up from toes, over feet to ankles; right over right, left over left, palms close to feet.

MONEY. Hold right hand, back to right, well out in front of right breast, index and thumb curved, forming an incomplete circle, space half inch beween tips, other fingers closed.

MONKEY (meaning: half white man, half dog). Pass the spread thumb and index finger of each hand, other fingers closed, over and near the surface of body from waist upwards, palms towards body; then make sign for WHITES; then pass the hand similarly from waist down, and make sign for DOG. The upper portion like white man, lower like dog.

MONTHS or MOONS. See pages 62 and 83 .

MOON (meaning: night sun). Make the sign for NIGHT; then with curved thumb and index of right hand form a segment or quarter moon, and hold it in line of vision to where moon should be on high.

MORNING. Make the signs for DAY and SUNRISE.

MOTHER. With partially curved compressed right hand give two or three gentle taps or pluckings at left breast.

MOTHER-IN-LAW. Make the sign for HUSBAND or WIFE, and then for MOTHER.

MOTION PICTURES. This is a strictly recent proposition, and must be so regarded. The modern Indian, however, knows all about the pictures, and thousands act in them. Have seen different descriptive signs made, the most common being to extend both flat hands, upright, and vibrate them rapidly, to show flicker of the picture, and sign LOOK. One Indian who had been to Hollywood made sign similar to OWL, as though looking into opera glass, and then sign for turning crank.

MOTOR CAR. Make the sign for automobile.

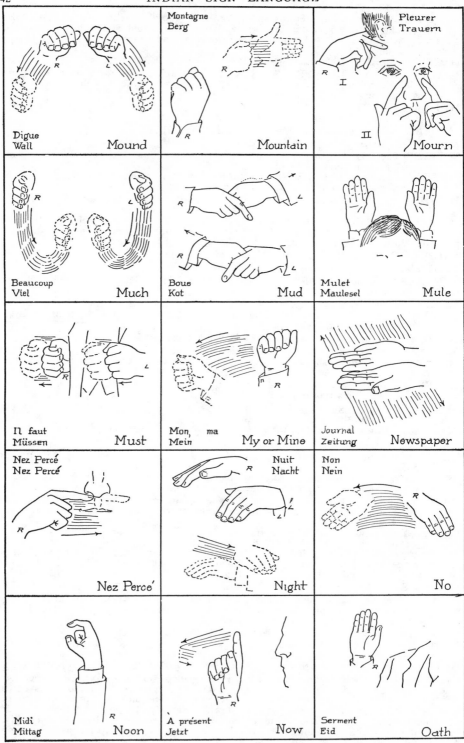

Digue
Wall   Mound

Montagne
Berg   Mountain

Pleurer
Trauern
I
II   Mourn

Beaucoup
Viel   Much

Boue
Kot   Mud

Mulet
Maulesel   Mule

Il faut
Müssen   Must

Mon, ma
Mein   My or Mine

Journal
Zeitung   Newspaper

Nez Percé
Nez Percé

Nez Perce'

Nuit
Nacht   Night

Non
Nein   No

Midi
Mittag   Noon

À présent
Jetzt   Now

Serment
Eid   Oath

Line drawing shows beginning and dotted outline shows end of movement of hands.
Students must Compare Each Diagram with Explanation Found on Opposite Page.

MOUND. Partially curve the hands and, with backs up, bring them alongside each other in front of body; separate the hands in downward curves, to right with right hand, to left with left.

MOUNTAIN. Push up the closed hand as in bluff, but raised higher; then make the sign for HARD. Use both hands to represent a mountainous country.

MOUNTAIN LION. Make the signs for CAT, for LONG TAIL, and for JUMP.

MOURN (meaning: cutting off the hair and crying). With extended separated right 2 hand make as though to cut off hair horizontally just below ears; then make the sign for CRY.

MOUSE. To represent height hold the right flat hand close to ground, and partially closing same hand imitate its movements in running; then make sign for NIGHT, and with right thumb and index nibble at left index.

MOVE (meaning: to move camp). Make sign for TEEPEE: then lower hands from this position as though taking down the lodge poles; then make the signs for WORK, for PACK, and GO.

MUCH. Make the sign for MANY.

MUD. With left compressed, catch or hold right compressed hand and drag down over same; then reverse and repeat (imitating an animal pulling its feet out of the mud); point to ground. For soft in any other sense, use signs for HARD and NO.

MULE. Hold extended hands alongside of ears, palms to front, fingers pointing upwards; by wrist action move hands forward and back to represent their motion.

MUST. Make the sign for PUSH. (Used as a command.)

MY or MINE. Make the sign for POSSESSION.

MYSTERIOUS or WONDERFUL. Make the sign for MEDICINE.

N

NAME. In asking the name of a person the Indian method would be to make the signs QUESTION, YOU, CALLED—"What are you called?" meaning: "What are you named?"

NARROW. Make the sign for FEW.

NAVAJO—Indian (meaning: makes striped blankets): Make the signs for WORK, BLANKET and STRIPED.

NEAR. Make the sign for CLOSE.

NEEDLE. Make the sign for SEW.

NEGRO (meaning: black white man). Make sign for WHITE MAN, and sign for BLACK.

NEW. Make the signs for OLD, NO, and GOOD.

NEWSPAPER. Hold the flat hands side by side, palm up; then move hands apart as though spread out, and sign LOOK. To this I have known an Indian to add the signs WRITING and TALK.

NEXT YEAR. You must indicate the season. If in winter you wish to say, "next summer," make signs for WINTER, for FINISHED, and for GRASS, showing high grass. If in Summer you wish to say, "next Winter," make signs for AUTUMN, for FINISHED, and for WINTER.

NEZ PERCÉ—Indian (meaning: pierced noses). Hold right index slightly under and to right of nose, then push index across to left below the nose.

NIGHT (meaning: earth covered over). Extend flat hands in front of body, ten inches apart, backs up, right hand a little higher; move right hand to left and left to right turning hands a trifle by wrist action.

NO. Hold extended flat right hand, back up, in front of body, fingers pointing to left and front; swing the hand to right and front while turning hand so that thumb is up and back downwards, then return to first position.

NOON. With right thumb and index forming incomplete circle one inch between tips, show position of sun overhead.

NOTIFY. Make the sign for TALK.

NOW. Bring extended index finger of right hand about 8 inches in front of face, and without stopping carry it quickly several inches to front, stopping with a rebound.

NUMBERS. See COUNT.

O

OATH. In early times there were several ways of imposing this obligation. Pointing to the zenith and the earth was an oath with many tribes. An ancient oath, with eyes and hands (flat) upraised, meant "God see my hands, they are clean." Holding up the right hand is now understood by all Indians, and is called "The white man's way."

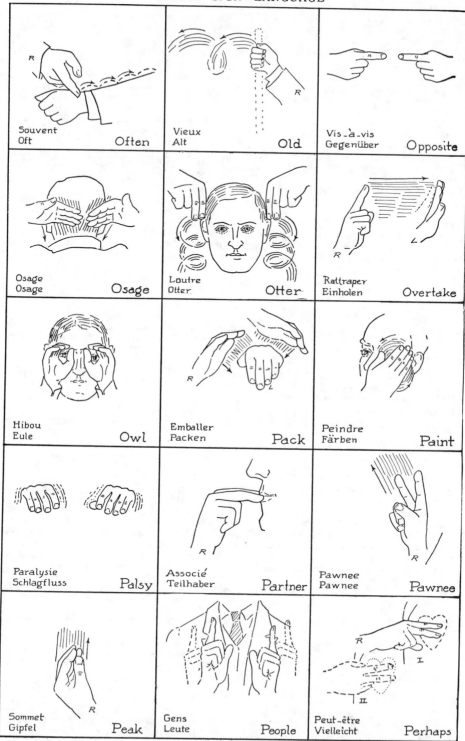

Souvent
Oft   Often

Vieux
Alt   Old

Vis_à_vis
Gegenüber   Opposite

Osage
Osage   Osage

Loutre
Otter   Otter

Rattraper
Einholen   Overtake

Hibou
Eule   Owl

Emballer
Packen   Pack

Peindre
Färben   Paint

Paralysie
Schlagfluss   Palsy

Associé
Teilhaber   Partner

Pawnee
Pawnee   Pawnee

Sommet
Gipfel   Peak

Gens
Leute   People

Peut_être
Vielleicht   Perhaps

Line drawing shows beginning and dotted outline shows end of movement of hands.
Students must Compare Each Diagram with Explanation Found on Opposite Page.

OBEY. Make the sign for LISTEN.

OCEAN. Make the signs for WATER and BIG.

OFFICER. Make the sign for CHIEF.

OFTEN (MANY TIMES, REPEAT). Hold left forearm horizontally in front of left breast, pointing to front; then with right index touch left forearm several times commencing at wrist and passing upwards towards elbow.

OJIBWAY. See CHIPPEWA.

OLD (meaning: walking with a stick). Hold closed right hand, back to right, twelve inches in front of right shoulder, at height of breast; move hand upwards, to front, downwards and back to first position in a curve. Repeat motion.

OPPOSITE. Point both extended index fingers toward each other, at same height, other fingers and thumbs closed.

OSAGE—Indian (meaning: shaved heads). Bring backs of extended hands alongside of head, fingers pointing to rear; move hands downwards as though cutting the hair with lower edges of hands. Repeat this.

OTTER (meaning: decorating the hair). Hold right hand near top of right ear, thumb, index and second fingers extended together; lower the hand while making a small spiral with tips of fingers. There is a general custom among all plains Indians of decorating the hair with strips of otter skin.

OUTSIDE. Make sign to show whether outside of teepee, house or camp; then with left hand still in position make sign for HERE with right hand, beyond or outside of the left hand.

OVER. Make the sign for ACROSS.

OVERTAKE. Extend left flat hand with palm outwards, fingers pointing to front and up; hold right 1 hand near breast, palm outwards, index pointing front and up; move right hand out till it touches left.

OWL (meaning: big eyes). Make sign for BIRD; then make circles of thumbs and indexes of both hands and place them in front of eyes.

OWN. Make the sign for POSSESSION.

P

PACK. Hold partly compressed left hand in front of body, back out; then with partly compressed right hand pat upper surface of left; then pat back of left; then reverse and in same manner pat right hand with left. This represents loading a pack animal.

PADDLE. Make the sign for BOAT, and indicate use of paddle.

PAINT. With fingers extended rub the cheeks and front of face with palm of right hand.

PALSY. Bring the hands close to breast, back up, then shake them with a quivering motion.

PARADE. Make sign for WHITE MAN, for SOLDIER, and for WALK. Sometimes add RIDING HORSEBACK, and GO.

PART. If one-half, make sign for HALF; if more or less indicate accordingly.

PARTNER. Make sign for BROTHER. Indians seem averse to partnership, but often adopt a man as friend or brother.

PAST. (Sense of time—meaning time behind.) Make the sign for BEFORE.

PAWNEE (meaning: Wolf). Make the sign for INDIAN, then hold right 2 hand, fingers extended, close to right shoulder, palm outwards; carry hand slightly upwards and six inches to front.

PAYMASTER. Make the signs for MONEY and CHIEF.

PEACE. Clasp the hands in front of body, with back of left hand down.

PEAK. Compress fingers of right hand tightly together, cone shape; then raise hand in front of body, back outwards.

PEOPLE. Right index, shoulder high, moving up and down as shown. Have seen Indians use both 5 hands, near breast, backs out.

PERHAPS (meaning: two hearts). Hold right 2 hand over heart, pointing to left, fingers separated; then by forearm movement roll the hand back and forth. When expressing many conflicting emotions or many doubts, vibrate or roll the extended 5 hand. This would represent deep consideration.

PHONOGRAPH. With right hand make as though to wind it up; then show turning disk; then make signs for LISTEN, and GOOD. (A flexible modern sign, well understood by Indians.)

PICKET—To picket a horse (meaning: to drive picket pin in the ground). Make the sign for HORSE, for WOOD; then bring closed left hand, thumb up, in front of body, and strike it a few times with closed right hand.

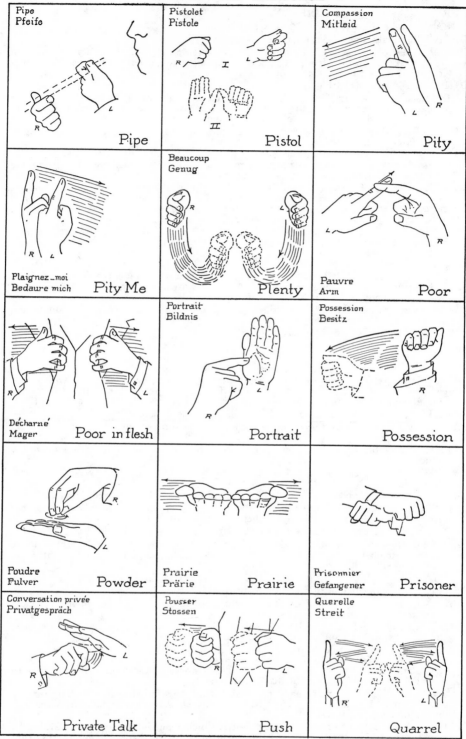

Pipe Pfeife	Pistolet Pistole	Compassion Mitleid
Pipe	Pistol	Pity
Plaignez _ moi Bedaure mich — Pity Me	Beaucoup Genug Plenty	Pauvre Arm — Poor
Décharné Mager — Poor in flesh	Portrait Bildnis Portrait	Possession Besitz Possession
Poudre Pulver — Powder	Prairie Prärie — Prairie	Prisonnier Gefangener — Prisoner
Conversation privée Privatgespräch — Private Talk	Pousser Stossen — Push	Querelle Streit — Quarrel

Line drawing shows beginning and dotted outline shows end of movement of hands.
Students must Compare Each Diagram with Explanation Found on Opposite Page.

PIPE (meaning: holding long wooden stem). Bring the hands in front of neck, backs down, left hand four inches from chin, right hand several inches in front of left; move hands to front and downwards short distance, as though lowering pipe; then repeat. (Stem is held between thumb and index.)

PISTOL. Make the sign for GUN; then with both hands indicate "six", for six shooter, by holding up right hand, fingers and thumb extended, separated, and holding up left thumb, left fingers closed.

PITY—towards another. Both 1 hands, backs up, carried outward and downward towards another person.

PITY ME. Hold both 1 hands, well out, and draw them to the breast.

PLANT. Make sign for CORN, for WORK; then with right hand near shoulder make as though dropping seed in the ground.

PLENTY. Hold extended 5 hands well out to right and left; then bring them in together as though gathering something up.

PONY. Make the signs for HORSE and LITTLE, showing height with left flat hand.

POOR (in possession). Hold up left 1 hand, back out, index pointed upwards; then with right index make as though to scrape left index bare, striking from tip of finger downwards.

POOR (meaning: flesh clawed off). Bring curved hands close to center of body and make as though to claw the flesh off the ribs, first with right then with left. Repeat.

PORCUPINE. Show size of animal; then point up with fingers as in grass; then indicate working on moccasin.

PORTRAIT. Hold left hand same as in MIRROR, and with right hand indicate as though making sketch on left palm.

POSSESSION (for such words as HIS, HERS, YOURS, MINE, etc). Hold closed fist in front of neck, back to right; swing hand slightly downwards and by wrist action have thumb point to front.

POWDER. Hold left flat hand in front of body, back down, and rub tips of fingers and thumb of right hand slightly above left palm.

PRAIRIE. Extend both hands out in front, about height of face, touching, palms up, fingers to front; then separate hands moving right to right, left to left on an even plane.

PRAIRIE DOG. To right of body hold right hand near ground, showing height of animal; then make sign for HOLE; then push compressed right hand through closed left hand, until tips emerge; then with thumb and index snap them as in LITTLE TALK, representing their chattering noise.

PRAY. Make the signs for WORK (meaning: making), and MEDICINE. Some Southern Indians hold both flat hands, palms up, high above the sides of the head—meaning: "God sees my hands; there is no blood on them, I am innocent."

PRESIDENT. Make the sign for WHITES, for CHIEF, and for BIG, and with left hand point afar as if towards Washington.

PRIEST (meaning: black robes). Make the sign for COAT, carrying hands well down, and for BLACK.
  The earliest Missionaries among the Indians were the Catholic Priests, known as "Black Robes," and Episcopalian ministers, known as "White Robes."

PRISONER (meaning: bound at wrists). Close the hands, cross the wrists in front of body, the right resting on left, palms down.

PRIVATE TALK. Hold extended left hand, back up, in front of left breast; with right thumb and index make sign for LITTLE TALK under and close to left palm.

PROUD. Used by Indians as meaning vain. Make sign for PAINT, for DRESS and for FOND—meaning, fond of GOOD DRESS.

PUEBLO—Indian. Make sign for INDIAN , for WORK, for BLANKET, and for STRIPED.

PUSH. Place both fists near breasts holding arms rigid; then move them a few inches forward as with an effort.

Q

QUARREL. Bring index fingers, pointing up, several inches apart, opposite each other, in front of body, level with shoulders; now by wrist action move right tip toward left, then tip toward right, alternately, and repeat. Make motions sharply. Also means SCOLDING.

QUEEN. Make signs for FEMALE, CHIEF, and BIG.

QUENCH. Make the sign for FIRE; then, with back up, hold extended right hand over place where sign for FIRE was made, and lower the hand; then make sign for WIPED OUT.

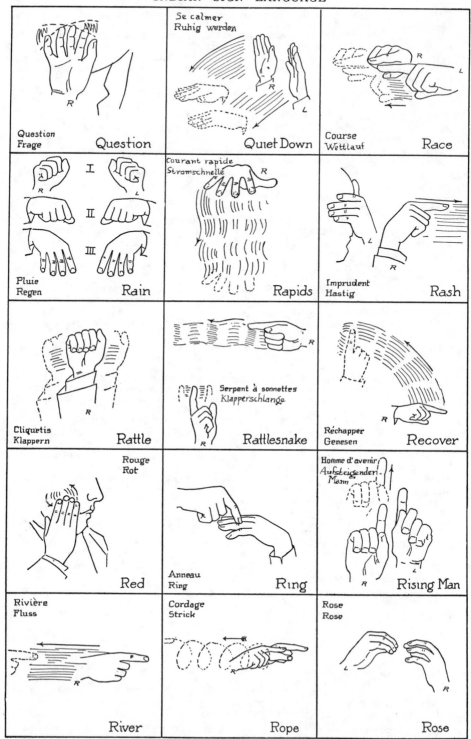

Question Frage **Question**	Se calmer Ruhig werden **Quiet Down**	Course Wettlauf **Race**
Pluie Regen **Rain**	Courant rapide Stromschnelle **Rapids**	Imprudent Hastig **Rash**
Cliquetis Klappern **Rattle**	Serpent à sonnettes Klapperschlange **Rattlesnake**	Réchapper Genesen **Recover**
Rouge Rot **Red**	Anneau Ring **Ring**	Homme d' avenir Aufsteigenden Mann **Rising Man**
Rivière Fluss **River**	Cordage Strick **Rope**	Rose Rose **Rose**

Line drawing shows beginning and dotted outline shows end of movement of hands.
Students must Compare Each Diagram with Explanation Found on Opposite Page.

QUESTION. Hold right 5 hand, palm outwards, at height of shoulders, fingers and
thumb extended, separated and pointing upwards, turn the hand slightly by wrist
action two or three times. If the person is distant, hold the hand higher and move
it considerably to right and left. This particularly means WHAT—and partially
means WHY, WHERE, WHEN; which see.

QUICK. Make the sign for HURRY.

QUIET DOWN. Hold flat hands, back up, out in front of body, as high as shoulders,
fingers pointing to front; lower the hands slowly.

R

RABBIT. Show the height of rabbit; then make the sign for JUMP.

RACE. State kind of race. Then move index fingers forward as in EQUAL.

RAILWAY. Make the sign for WAGON; then for FIRE with right hand held well
up in front of head, then sign FAST.

RAIN (meaning: falling from clouds). In front of head hold closed hands, near each
other, backs up, in same relative positions; lower hands a trifle by wrist action,
and while doing so open the hands. Repeat motion twice, slowly.

RAINBOW. Make the sign for RAIN, and for FINISHED; then with extended right
hand, back up, imitate circle of rainbow in sky.

RAPIDS. Make the sign for RIVER and for ROCK; then hold right 5 hand near
breast, pointing downwards; with tremulous motion move hand quickly to front
and down.

RASH. Hold the left flat hand over the eyes, then thrust the right index outward
from back of left hand.

RATTLE. With closed right hand held in front and above right shoulder, shake the
hand as if it was a rattle. (The rattle is an important musical instrument in Indian
ceremonies.)

RATTLESNAKE. Make the sign for SNAKE; then extend right index upwards in
front of right shoulder and vibrate sharply.

REACH (to). See ARRIVE THERE.

READING. Make signs for BOOK and LOOK.

RECEIVE. Make the sign for POSSESSION.

RECOVER. Place right 1 hand before right breast, back up, forearm horizontal;
raise the hand until forearm straight up, turning hand until back is to front. This
means recovery from sickness or escape from danger.

RED (meaning: paint used on face). With fingers pointing upward, rub right cheek
with inside first joints of right hand, making circular motion.

REMAIN. Make the sign for SIT.

REMEMBER. Make the signs for HEART, and KNOW.

REPEAT. Make the sign for OFTEN.

RESTRAIN. Make the sign for HOLD, and for KEEP QUIET.

RETREAT. Make the sign for CHARGE, to show the attack; then by wrist action
turn the hands so that fingers point to rear.

RICH. Make the signs for POSSESS, MANY, PONIES (or HORSES).

RIDE. If animal is meant, make the sign for HORSE, and then move hands forward
in small curves. If riding a vehicle make the sign for same, and then make sign
for SIT on left palm.

RING (finger). Hold left 5 hand in front of breast, lying flat, back up; then touch back
of finger on third joint with right index.

RISING MAN. Make sign for person; then hold left hand at height of neck, palm
outwards, index pointing upwards; bring extended index of right hand beside and
lower than left; raise right slowly until well above other hand.

RIVER (meaning: water flowing). Make the sign for water; then move right hand
to left of face, height of neck, index extended pointing left, move hand to right
until opposite right shoulder, with index horizontal.

ROAD. With both open hand palms up, alternately push hands back and forth. A
modern sign gives TRAIL and WAGON.

ROCK. Make the sign for HARD, and indicate shape.

ROPE. Hold hands as in AFTER; then with tip of right index make a spiral curve
by wrist action while drawing right hand to rear.

ROSE. Hold slightly compressed left hand out in front; then with right compressed
pluck at ends of fingers.

RUN (to). Make the sign for WALK and for FAST.

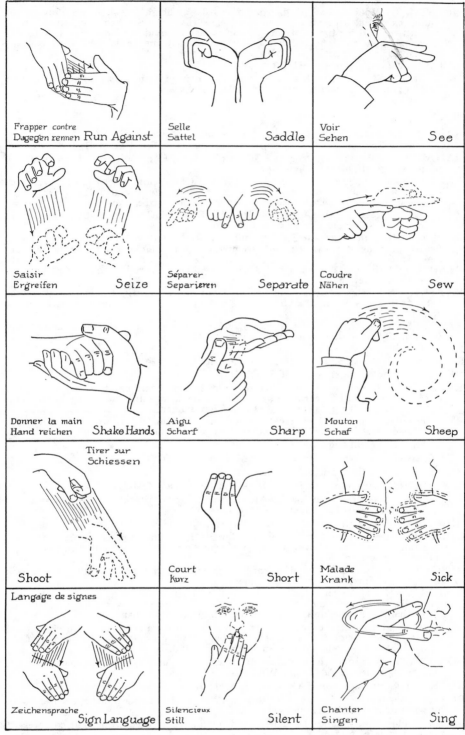

Frapper contre
Dagegen rennen Run Against

Selle
Sattel   Saddle

Voir
Sehen   See

Saisir
Ergreifen   Seize

Séparer
Separieren   Separate

Coudre
Nähen   Sew

Donner la main
Hand reichen   Shake Hands

Aigu
Scharf   Sharp

Mouton
Schaf   Sheep

Tirer sur
Schiessen

Shoot

Court
Kurz   Short

Malade
Krank   Sick

Langage de signes

Zeichensprache Sign Language

Silencieux
Still   Silent

Chanter
Singen   Sing

Line drawing shows beginning and dotted outline shows end of movement of hands
Students must Compare Each Diagram with Explanation Found on Opposite Page.

RUN AGAINST. Hold flat left hand in front of breast, back out; hold right in same relative position but nearer body; move right briskly so that back strikes inside of left hand.

S

SACRED. Make the sign for MEDICINE.

SAD (meaning: heart laid on the ground). Make the sign for HEART; then swing hand out and downwards toward the ground, turning palm up.

SADDLE. Place inside of both wrists together in front of breast; then holding this position, push both closed hands as far back as possible.

SALT. Touch the tongue with tip of extended right index, other fingers and thumb closed; then make the sign for BAD. Sometimes the sign for WHITE is made.

SAME. Make the sign for EQUAL.

SERGEANT. Make the sign for WHITES, for SOLDIER, and with right index mark position, extent and number of stripes on the arms.

SAW. Imitate using the tool.

SCHOOL HOUSE. Make the sign for HOUSE, for WHITES, for LOOK (2 fingers pointing towards left palm), and for KNOW.

SCOLD. Make the signs for TALK and BAD.

SCOUT. Make the sign for WOLF.

SCOUT (to). Make the sign for WOLF; then sign for LOOK.

SEARCH. See SCOUT.

SEASONS. The usual names for the seasons are WINTER, SPRING, SUMMER, FALL, and for explanation of same see pages 61, 53, 55, 27.

SEE. Bring right 2 hand to opposite eyes, and the two fingers should point in the direction one is looking.

SEIZE. Move open hands out in front of body; close them briskly and draw towards body, as though seizing something.

SELL. See EXCHANGE.

SEPARATE. Hold the 1 hands close together in front, indexes pointing forward; by wrist action turn the hands so that right index points to right and front, left index to left and front; moving right hand to right and front, left to left and front.

SEW. Hold flat left hand, back to left, in front of body; use right index as an awl or needle, bringing it just over thumb, pointing to left, inner surface pressed against inner surface of index; move right hand slightly to left, and by wrist action turn back of index down as it passes. Repeat motion two or three times.

SHAKE HANDS. Clasp hands in front of body. In former times Indians only clasped hands in concluding a treaty or making peace. They now, in dealing with whites, observe the custom.

SHARP. Hold flat right hand, back down, in front of right breast; then lightly touch lower edge of right hand with ball of left thumb; then make sign for GOOD.

SHAWL. Make sign for FEMALE; then sign for BLANKET.

SHE. Make the sign for WOMAN.

SHEEP—Mountain (meaning; horns). Compress and slightly curve the hands in front and above the head—have them curve in a way similar to that made by the big horns of the sheep.

SHEEP—Domestic. Make sign for MOUNTAIN SHEEP, for WHITES, and for WITH.

SHOE. Make the signs for MOCCASIN and WHITES.

SHOOT. Hold nearly closed right hand, back up, in front of breast, tips of first three fingers pressed against ball of thumb; move hand out, down and to left, while snapping the fingers out from under the thumb.

SHORT. Hold compressed right hand to right and front of body, fingers pointing upward and hand at height to be represented.

SHOSHONE—Indian (meaning: sheep eater). Make the sign for INDIAN, for SHEEP, and for EAT.

SICK. Hold extended 5 hands in front of body; then wave them out and in, two or three times, to denote throbbing.

SIGN LANGUAGE. Hold out flat left hand, back up, touch back of fingers with inside of fingers of right hand; then reverse this process; then make sign for TALK.

SILENT. Place tips of fingers of right hand over lips, and incline the head slightly to front.

SILVER. Make the signs for MONEY and WHITE.

SINCE. See AFTER.

SING. Hold right 2 hand in front of mouth and make sign for ALL.

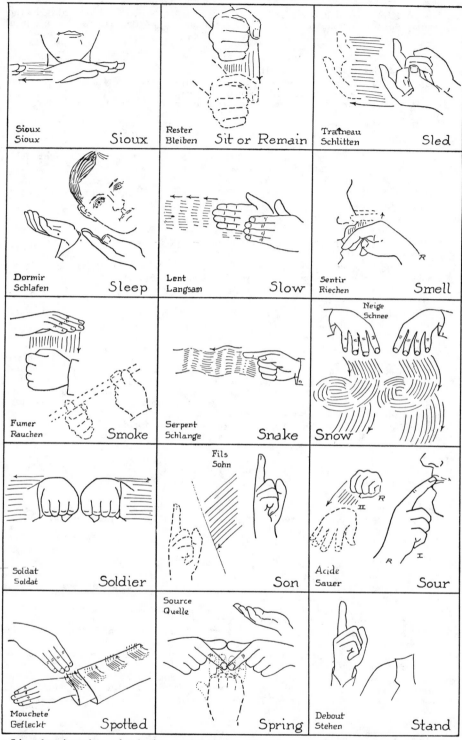

Sioux Sioux Sioux	Rester Bleiben Sit or Remain	Traîneau Schlitten Sled
Dormir Schlafen Sleep	Lent Langsam Slow	Sentir Riechen Smell
Fumer Rauchen Smoke	Serpent Schlange Snake	Neige Schnee Snow
Soldat Soldat Soldier	Fils Sohn Son	Acide Sauer Sour
Moucheté Gefleckt Spotted	Source Quelle Spring	Debout Stehen Stand

Line drawing shows beginning and dotted outline shows end of movement of hands.
Students must Compare Each Diagram with Explanation Found on Opposite Page.

SIOUX—Indian (meaning: cutting off heads). Draw right flat hand across, from left, in front of neck as though cutting off the head. This is the sign of the Sioux or Dakota Nation.

SISTER. Make the sign for FEMALE; then place the tips of extended index and second finger against lips, fingers horizontal, backs up, other fingers and thumb closed; move the hand horizontally several inches to the front.

SISTER-IN-LAW. Make the sign for BROTHER, for HIS, and for WIFE.

SIT or REMAIN. Hold closed right hand in front of and little below right shoulder; then move hand downward several inches.

SLED. Hold the 1 hands, backs down, in front of body, equally advanced, several inches apart, indexes curved, move hands forward simultaneously.

SLEEP. Lower the extended flat hands with a sweep into following position: left hand in front of right breast pointing to right, right hand six inches to right of left, pointing to front and right; then incline head to right.

SLOW. With both palms facing and three inches apart, move hands slowly forward by short stops.

SMALL. If referring to an animal, indicate the height. For small quantity of anything make the sign for FEW.

SMELL. Bring right 2 hand, fingers separated, back up, in front of chin pointing to face; then by wrist action move the hand upwards, so that nose passes between tips of fingers.

SMOKE. For distant or signal fire smoke, make sign for FIRE, and continue raising hand until higher than head.

SMOKE (meaning: to smoke a pipe). Hold left fist in front of body; then with flat right hand held three inches above left strike down two or three times; then make sign for PIPE.

SMOOTH. Make the sign for PRAIRIE, and add ROCK or BLUFF, and WIPED OUT.

SNAKE. Hold right 1 hand at right side, waist high, move hand one foot forward with a wavy motion.

SNOW. Hold extended 5 hands in front of face, fingers pointing downward, lower in circular zigzags, to indicate whirling, sifting snow.

SNOW SHOE. Indicate the shape and size with right index; then make signs for WALK, SNOW, and GOOD.

SOAP. With hands held in front of body, rub them together as though washing them.

SOFT. Make the signs for HARD and NO.

SOLDIER. Bring closed fists in front of breast, thumbs touching; then separate hands horizontally to right and left.

SON. Make sign for man; then with right index pointing upwards, lower hand to indicate height of child.

SORREL. Touch something yellow and make sign for LITTLE.

SOUR. With tip of extended index of right hand touch the tongue; then make sign for BAD.

SPEAK. See TALK.

SPOON. Make the sign for BUFFALO, and leaving right hand in position touch it with left; then use right hand to dip into some vessel, and carry to mouth.

SPOTTED. Hold out flat left hand and arm, pointing right and front; then hold right hand above left wrist, fingers slightly separated; then with right finger tips starting at left wrist, touch left forearm every two inches towards elbow, merely brushing with ends of fingers. Southern Indians lay back of hands on each other, fingers over fingers, then rub them back and forth several times, to represent spotted, mottled, brindle, roan, or any off color.

SPRING (meaning: grass coming out of ground). Make the signs for GRASS and LITTLE.

SPRING (meaning: a spring of water). Make the sign for WATER; then with thumbs and index fingers form a circle in front of body; then, still holding left in position, bring compressed right under the circle, fingers held under the thumb; then release them with a snap to indicate bubbling spring. Repeat last movement.

SPY. Make the sign for WOLF.

STAND. To indicate anything standing upright, bring right 1 hand to right and front and higher than right shoulder, index pointing upwards.

STANDING ROCK (meaning: an agency on the MISSOURI RIVER). Make the signs for STAND and ROCK.

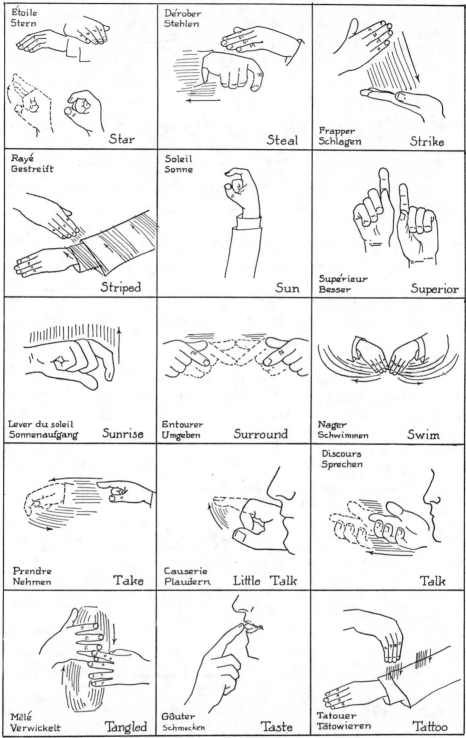

Étoile
Stern

Star

Dérober
Stehlen

Steal

Frapper
Schlagen

Strike

Rayé
Gestreift

Striped

Soleil
Sonne

Sun

Supérieur
Besser

Superior

Lever du soleil
Sonnenaufgang Sunrise

Entourer
Umgeben Surround

Nager
Schwimmen Swim

Prendre
Nehmen Take

Causerie
Plaudern Little Talk

Discours
Sprechen

Talk

Mêlé
Verwickelt Tangled

Goûter
Schmecken Taste

Tatouer
Tätowieren Tattoo

Line drawing shows beginning and dotted outline shows end of movement of hands.
Students must Compare Each Diagram with Explanation Found on Opposite Page.

STAR. Make the sign for NIGHT; then form a small incomplete circle with right thumb and index, and raise hand toward sky. For brilliant star, snap index against thumb to denote twinkling.

START. Make the sign for GO.

STAY. Make the sign for SIT.

STEAL. Hold extended left hand in front of left breast, back up, pass right 1 hand under and close to left hand, until right wrist is close to left palm, right index extended; then draw back the right hand, at same time crooking index.

STEAMBOAT (meaning: fire-boat). Make the sign for BOAT; then sign for FIRE, holding hand a little higher than the head.

STINGY. Make the signs for HEART and FEW.

STONE. Make the sign for HARD, and indicate shape as of a boulder.

STOP. See HALT.

STORE. Make signs for HOUSE and TRADE.

STRAIGHT. See TRUE.

STRIKE. Hold left flat hand out in front of left breast, back down; use right hand like a hatchet and strike palm of left. Generally used to represent a blow given with a weapon.

STRIPED. Hold left arm as in SPOTTED; then draw palm of extended right hand from left to right across left forearm in various places.

STRONG. The sign for BRAVE was formerly used by many. The later preference is to hold right fist above left fist and strike over and downwards with twisting motion, as though breaking a small stick.

SUGAR. Touch the tongue with tip of right index; then make the sign for GOOD.

SUMMER. Make the sign for GRASS, holding hands very high. Some Indians also denote SUN passing overhead, and HOT.

SUN. Form, with index and thumb of right hand, an incomplete circle, space of one inch between tips; hold hand towards the east; then move it in a curve across the heavens towards the west. Also used to denote the time of day. (Right hand held towards left indicates eastward).

SUNDAY. Make signs for DAY and MEDICINE. Have seen Indians describe other days of the week by indicating so many days before or after Medicine Day.

SUNRISE. With right index and thumb make an incomplete circle, other fingers closed. Hold arm horizontal pointing to left; then raise hand about a foot.

SUNSET—Opposite to SUNRISE. With thumb and index of right hand forming an incomplete circle, extend right hand to right, about 1 foot above horizontal; then lower same 12 inches.

SUPERIOR. In comparing two persons or things, place the two extended indexes side by side, pointing up, one held higher than the other, the highest representing the superior. When one is superior to several, place index of right hand above extended thumb and four fingers of left.

SUPPER. See EAT.

SURPRISE. Make the sign for ASTONISH.

SURROUND. Hold thumbs and indexes in semi-circle several inches apart and opposite each other; then bring them together to form a flat circle.

SWEET. See SUGAR.

SWIM. Make the sign for WATER; then strike the arms out well in front as though swimming.

T

TAIL. Place right 1 hand to rear of center of body, index finger pointing to rear and downwards.

TAKE. Push the right 1 hand well out in front, to right of body, index extended, pointing to front; pull hand quickly towards body while curving index finger into a hook.

TALK. A "little talk", or "one person talking to another", is expressed as follows: with nail of right index pressing against thumb, move hand a trifle to front and snap the index straight forward (these words "are thrown out"). Repeat motion. For a council to "speak at length", hold right flat hand, back down, in front of mouth, and move hand outward a few inches; repeating the motion.

TALL. Hold right hand as in STAND, but at full length of extended arm.

TANGLED. Move the hands, one about the other, with fingers slightly separated.

TASTE. Touch the tongue with tip of right index.

TATTOO. Compress the right hand, and tap with ends of fingers that portion of body which has been marked.

TEA. Make the sign for TREE, for LEAF, for DRINK, and for GOOD.

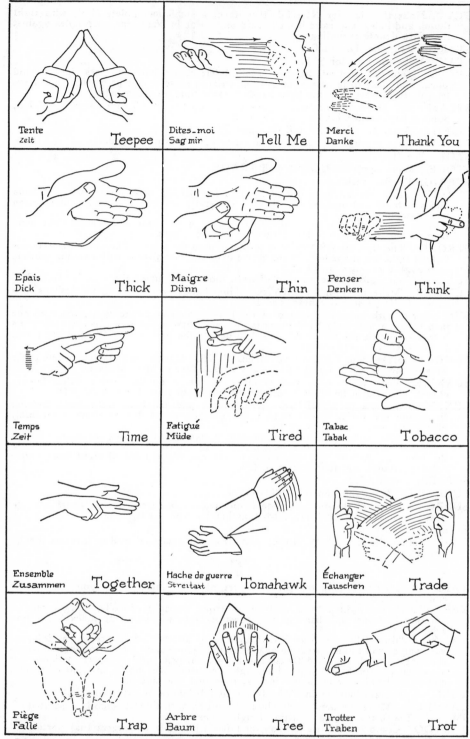

Tente Zelt Teepee	Dites_moi Sag mir Tell Me	Merci Danke Thank You
Épais Dick Thick	Maigre Dünn Thin	Penser Denken Think
Temps Zeit Time	Fatigué Müde Tired	Tabac Tabak Tobacco
Ensemble Zusammen Together	Hache de guerre Streitaxt Tomahawk	Échanger Tauschen Trade
Piège Falle Trap	Arbre Baum Tree	Trotter Traben Trot

Line drawing shows beginning and dotted outline shows end of movement of hands.
Students must Compare Each Diagram with Explanation Found on Opposite Page.

TEEPEE. With index fingers, touching at tips, form an angle of 60 degress. Sometimes index fingers are crossed at first joints, to indicate extended teepee poles.

TELEGRAPH. Make sign for WRITE; then hold flat hand back out, in front of breast; with lower edge of extended right hand strike upper edge of left, with a rebound, and then make sign for GO, quickly. A flexible modern sign.

TELL ME—TALK TO ME (meaning bring the word to me). The open right hand is placed palm up in front of mouth; then draw toward the lips with a quick jerk.

THANK YOU. Extend both flat hands, backs up, in sweeping curve outward and downward, toward another person.

THERE. Make the sign for SIT, moving the hand well out from body. Have seen Indians simply point with middle finger.

THEY or THEM. Point to person and make sign ALL.

THICK. Hold up flat left hand sideways in front of breast, with right hand reach around from below and clasp thickest part; move thumb and finger back and forth few times.

THIEF. Make the sign for PERSON and for STEAL.

THIN. If possible point to something thin; otherwise with right thumb and two fingers rub lower edge of left hand just back of little finger. This is a somewhat confusing sign, as it also stands for BACON. If making sign for BACON, add the sign EAT.

THINK (meaning: drawn from the heart). Hold right hand, back up, against left breast, index extended and pointing to left; move hand horizontally outwards eight or ten inches, turning palm downward.

THOUSAND. Make sign for HUNDRED and for TEN.

THREAD. As though twisting thread rub inner surface of tips of thumb and index; make the sign for SEW, ending by carrying right hand well out to right to imitate motion of sewing.

THUNDER. Make the sign for BIRD, and for FIRE, holding the hand a little in front of and higher than head. (Indian lore records thunder as being caused by the "Thunder Bird".)

TIME. There has been some diversity of gesture in regard to passage of time, but we present the most logical. For abstract TIME, extend right and left 1 hands towards the left, hands tandem, then pull right hand about three inches backward to right. See BEFORE, AFTER, FUTURE, PAST, BEHIND and LONG TIME.

TIMOROUS. Make the signs for COWARD, and LITTLE.

TIRED. Hold out 1 hands together, backs up; lower hands a few inches while drawing them slightly towards body.

TOBACCO. Hold the flat left hand, back down, in front of body; place lower edge, or heel, of closed right hand on left palm; then with heel of right hand rub left palm with a circular motion.

TODAY. Make the signs for DAY and NOW. Many Indians merely use NOW.

TOGETHER. Make the sign for WITH.

TOMAHAWK. Generally indicated by using right forearm and hand as a hatchet, by elbow action, striking forward and downward with flat hand held edgewise.

TOMORROW. Make the sign for NIGHT, then sign for DAY; then with left hand indicate SUN rising in east.

TONGUE. Protrude tongue a trifle and touch with first finger.

TORNADO (meaning: the wind charges). Make the sign for WIND, and for CHARGE.

TOWN. Make signs for CITY and LITTLE.

TRACK. Make the sign for WALK and point to the ground.

TRADE. Make the sign for EXCHANGE.

TRADER. Make the signs for WHITES, CHIEF and TRADE.

TRAIL (to). Make the signs for TRACK and LOOK.

TRAP. For iron or steel traps, touch or point to something made of metal; hold closed hands side by side, knuckles touching, index fingers curved and touching; then bring sides of indexes together, to represent closing of jaws of trap.

TREATY. If the treaty is between two tribes make the signs for MAKE, SMOKE, and SHAKE HANDS. If treaty is with the whites, make signs for SHAKE HANDS and WRITE.

TREE. Hold open left hand about ten inches in front of shoulder, back outward, thumb and fingers spread. Move slightly upward, slowly, to indicate growth.

TROT. Make sign for the animal; then bring both fists in front of body, same height, equally advanced, and few inches apart; then imitate action of front feet in trotting by alternately striking to front and downwards.

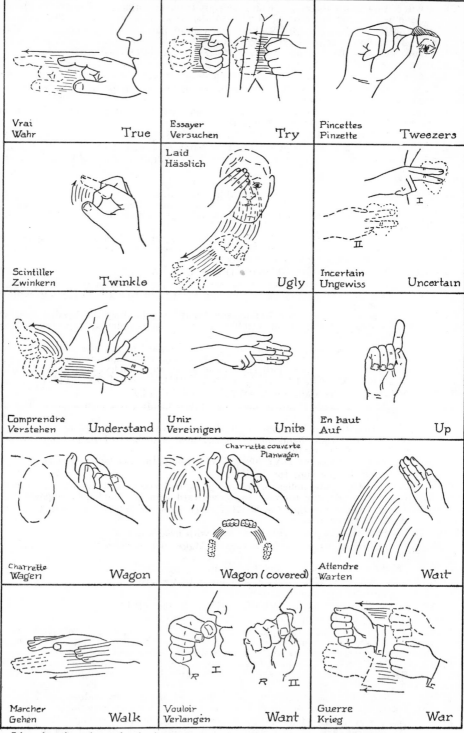

Vrai
Wahr — True

Essayer
Versuchen — Try

Pincettes
Pinzette — Tweezers

Scintiller
Zwinkern — Twinkle

Laid
Hässlich — Ugly

Incertain
Ungewiss — Uncertain

Comprendre
Verstehen — Understand

Unir
Vereinigen — Unite

En haut
Auf — Up

Charrette
Wagen — Wagon

Charrette couverte
Planwagen — Wagon (covered)

Attendre
Warten — Wait

Marcher
Gehen — Walk

Vouloir
Verlangen — Want

Guerre
Krieg — War

Line drawing shows beginning and dotted outline shows end of movement of hands.
Students must Compare Each Diagram with Explanation Found on Opposite Page.

TROUBLE. Make sign for HEART; then hold right 5 hand over heart, palm almost touching, and by wrist action vibrate as in PERHAPS.

TRUE (meaning; one way or tongue straight). Hold right 1 hand, back up, under chin, close to neck; move index finger straight to the front. This means straight from heart and tongue.

TRY. Make the sign for PUSH.

TURKEY (meaning: beard). Make the sign for BIRD; then place compressed right hand under chin, pointing downwards; vibrate hand slightly by wrist action.

TWEEZERS. With tip of thumb and index, make as though same were a small pair of tweezers; then indicate pulling out hair from face or eyebrows with a jerk. This is a constant practice with Indians.

TWINKLE. Make the sign for STAR, and while holding hand in that position snap index and thumb as in LITTLE TALK.

U

UGLY. Pass the palm of flat right hand in a circle close to face; then make the sign for BAD.

UNCERTAIN. Make the sign for PERHAPS.

UNDECIDED. Make the sign for PERHAPS.

UNDERSTAND. Make the sign for KNOW.

UNITE. Make the sign for WITH.

UNLUCKY. Make the signs for MEDICINE and BAD.

UP. Point upward with right index.

US. Make the signs for ME, ALL.

UTE—Indian. Make sign for INDIAN and for BLACK, and rub the face as in RED.

V

VACCINATE. Make the signs for WHITES, MEDICINE, MAN, and with extended right index finger strike left arm between shoulder and elbow.

VIGILANT. Make sign for LOOK, pointing in different directions and moving hand rapidly; then signs MUCH, SLEEP, NO.

VILLAGE. Make sign for TEEPEE, and for MANY.

W

WAGON (meaning: wheels). Hold hands, backs down, at equal distance in front of body, four inches apart, index fingers curved, others and thumb closed; indicate motion of wheels by making small circle with indexes.

WAGON (COVERED). Make the sign for WAGON; then hold both flat hands, backs up, indexes touching, height of face, and sweep them out and down in a curve to indicate wagon top.

WAGON-ROAD. Make the signs for ROAD and WAGON.

WAIT. Make sign for HALT, but more gently and not stopping abruptly. Repeat gesture.

WALK (meaning: motion of feet). For a person, hold flat hands in front of body equally advanced; move right to front, upwards and downwards describing an oval circle; move left to front in same way; as left is brought down draw right hand to rear and repeat first motion, thereby alternating the motions of the feet. For an animal, close the hands and make same motions as above.

WANT (meaning: give me). Hold the right hand close to chin back to right, form an unclosed circle with thumb and index, back of index at height of mouth, half inch space between tips of index and thumb, plane of circle vertical; move hand in slight curve downwards, outwards and upwards; turning hand by wrist action, ending with little finger as high as index.

WAR. Make the sign for FIGHT.

WAR BONNET. Carry the flat hands from front to rear, close to sides of head, fingers pointing upwards, palms toward head; then carry right hand from top of head well down to rear of body.

WAR-CLUB. Show the size of war-club stone; denote rawhide covering of handle by clasping left index with right hand; then strike to front and down with right hand.

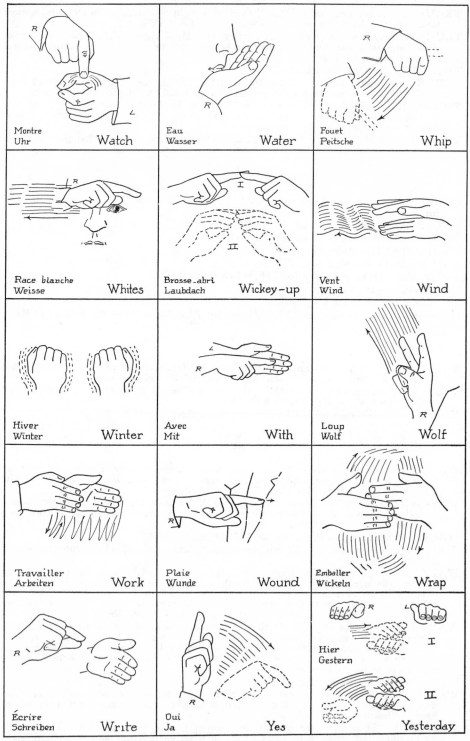

Montre Uhr **Watch**	Eau Wasser **Water**	Fouet Peitsche **Whip**
Race blanche Weisse **Whites**	Brosse-abri Laubdach **Wickey-up**	Vent Wind **Wind**
Hiver Winter **Winter**	Avec Mit **With**	Loup Wolf **Wolf**
Travailler Arbeiten **Work**	Plaie Wunde **Wound**	Emballer Wickeln **Wrap**
Écrire Schreiben **Write**	Oui Ja **Yes**	Hier Gestern **Yesterday**

Line drawing shows beginning and dotted outline shows end of movement of hands.
Students must Compare Each Diagram with Explanation Found on Opposite Page.

WAR-DANCE. Make the signs for WAR, and DANCE.

WARRIOR. Make the signs for MAN, and WAR.

WASH. Make the sign for WATER; then by motions imitate the act of washing.

WASTE. See DESTROY.

WATCH. With thumb and index of left hand form a horizontal circle; then hold right index over same and move tip around the indicated circle; make sign for LOOK pointing at circle; make sign for KNOW, and for SUN—all of which indicates size of watch, movement of hands—by looking at same you will know where the Sun is.

WATER (meaning: drinking out of palm of hand). Hold the cupped right hand, back down, in front of and little above mouth; fingers pointing to left and upwards; then move hand downwards, turning palm towards mouth. At end of RIVER or LAKE some Indians make the sign of dipping a handful of water with right cupped hand, held waist high.

WE. Make the signs for I or ME and ALL.

WEAK. Make signs for STRONG and NO.

WHEN. Make the sign for QUESTION, for HOW MANY, and indicate whether SLEEPS, MOONS, or WINTERS.

WHERE (meaning: what point). Make the sign for QUESTION, then point with right index in different directions.

WHIP. With closed right hand strike from front to right and rear, as though riding a horse and whipping him with a quirt.

WHISKEY. Make the signs for FIRE and WATER.

WHITE. Make the sign for COLOR; then rub with tip of right index the small segment at upper end of left thumb nail, or point to something white.

WHITES (meaning: cap wearers). Hold right hand to left of face on level of eyes, back up, index pointing to left; draw hand over to right side, index finger passing across above the eyes.

WHITE MAN. Make the sign for WHITES and for MAN.

WHY. Make the sign for INTERROGATE or QUESTION, but turn the hand very slowly.

WICKEY-UP. Hold hands several inches apart in front of body, indexes extended and lapping; from this position change the hands, back up, edges pointing to front, fingers separated and slightly curved, move hands downward on curve.

WIFE. Make the signs for FEMALE and MARRY.

WILD. Make the sign for BY ITSELF.

WILL (meaning: I will). Make the sign for PUSH.

WIND. Hold the hands with backs in, near body at height of shoulders, and with wavy motion move the hands in direction of the wind.

WINTER. Hold up the closed hands in front of body, forearms vertical, hands several inches apart; then give a shivering, tremulous motion to hands. With most Indians a year is called a winter, or one cold.

WIPED OUT. See EXTERMINATE.

WISE (meaning: heart and head both good). Make the sign for HEART, touch forehead, and make sign for GOOD.

WITH. Hold flat left hand, back to left, in front; bring side of extended right index against center of left palm, index pointing to front.

WOLF. Hold the right hand with palm outwards near right shoulder, first and second fingers extended and separated and pointing up; move the hand several inches to front and upwards.

WOMAN. Make the sign for FEMALE and indicate height.

WONDERFUL or MYSTERIOUS. Make the sign for MEDICINE.

WOOD. Make the signs for TREE and CHOP.

WOODPECKER. Make the sign for BIRD; then hold left forearm about vertical in front of left shoulder; now bring partially compressed right hand and place it near elbow of left forearm, right side; move hand with a jump to left side; then to little higher up, showing manner of hopping around a tree; then lower left hand and tap palm several times with tip of curved index of right hand.

WORK. Bring flat hands in front of body edgewise, few inches apart, right hand higher and back of left; then raise and lower the hands by wrist action, to indicate working.

WOUND. Hold right 1 hand in front of body; move hand briskly towards body, turning index finger to left or right so that it grazes surface of body.

WRAP. Bring slightly compressed hands, backs outward, in front of body, backs of
    fingers of right hand resting against palm of left, fingers horizontal; then move
    hands around each other in rotary motion.

WRITE. Hold flat left hand, back to front and down, out in front of body, fingers
    pointing to right; then as if with pencil between thumb and index of right hand,
    make as though writing on left palm.

Y

YEAR. Make the sign for WINTER, for this year add sign for NOW.

YELLOW. Make the sign for COLOR; then point to something yellow.

YES (meaning: bowing the head and body). Hold right hand, back to right, in front
    of right breast, height of shoulder, index extended and pointing upwards, other
    fingers nearly closed, thumb resting on side of second finger; move the hand slightly
    to left and a little downwards, at same time closing index over thumb.

YESTERDAY. Make sign for NIGHT; then, still holding left hand in position, sweep
    the right upwards and to right in a semi-circle, until it is at same height as left
    hand, terminating with back of hand down.

YOU. Point right 1 hand at person addressed.

YOUR or YOURS. Point to person indicated and make sign for POSSESSION.

ONE WAY TO TELL YOUR NAME AND WHERE YOU LIVE

The names of Indians were denoted by natural objects, birds, animals, etc., and were readily expressed
in gesture. The writer has been asked how he would express the name "John Smith" in sign language. It was
an Indian who suggested a good way whereby people of different tongues can tell each other their names and
where they live. This is by asking as follows:—"What is your name? Where do you live? Write it." Which
in the sign language would be:—QUESTION YOU CALLED, QUESTION YOU SIT, WRITE.

As practically everybody can read and write they can in this way introduce themselves, and, after this,
further conversation in sign is easy. This is of particular value to Boy Scouts of different tongues, as at
the Jamboree.

We know of many Boy Scouts who adopt Indian names, for use in their games, ceremonials, and
conversation.

INDIAN MOONS OR MONTHS

This work would be incomplete without some reference and information regarding
the Indian "moons" or months.

We have approached this subject with hesitation, because the Indian moons cor-
respond only in a general way to our own months and with certain tribes the names vary
greatly.

The following moons, or months, are those adopted by the American Indian Association after careful study, and are approved as being most nearly correct by Dr. Charles
Eastman, Strong Wolf, Running Bear and other prominent Indians. Where two or
more names are given for the same month, we have selected the one which can be gestured and pictured most easily, and is most generally used.

JANUARY. Snow Moon (or Cold Moon), make signs for MOON and SNOW.

FEBRUARY. Hunger Moon; make signs for MOON and HUNGRY.

MARCH. Crow Moon (Awaking Moon or Warm Moon); make signs for MOON,
    BIRD and BLACK.

APRIL. Grass Moon (Geese Moon); make signs for MOON and GRASS.

MAY. Planting Moon (Flower Moon); make signs for MOON, DIG and GROW.

JUNE. Rose Moon (Buck Moon); make signs for MOON and ROSE.

JULY. Heat Moon (Blood Moon); make signs for MOON, SUN and HOT.

AUGUST. Thunder Moon (Sturgeon Moon); make signs for MOON and THUNDER.

SEPTEMBER. Hunting Moon (Corn Festival Moon); make signs for MOON and
    HUNT.

OCTOBER. Falling Leaf Moon (Traveling Moon); make signs for MOON and LEAF,
    with a falling motion.

NOVEMBER. Beaver Moon (Mad Moon); make signs for MOON and BEAVER..

DECEMBER. Long Night Moon; make signs for MOON, NIGHT, and LONG TIME.

NOTE: The meaning and derivation of our common month names may be of interest
for comparison: 1. January; Janus, a two-faced God. 2. February; To purify. 3. March;
Mars, God of War. 4. April; Aperio, to open. 5. May; Maia, Goddess of Growth.
6. June; Junius, a Roman Gentile name. 7. July; for Julius Caesar. 8. August; for
Augustus Caesar. 9. September; seventh month. 10. October; eighth month. 11.
November; ninth month. 12. December; tenth month.

SIGN LANGUAGE SIMPLIFIED

The Indian Sign Language is the world's most easily learned language because it is elemental, basic, logical, and the signs in general are what should properly be made to illustrate the idea—the language being largely idiomatic—conveying ideas.

When you beckon with your finger you are saying the word COME; when you wave your hand outwards you say GO. When you point upwards with your index finger you say UP. When you point downwards you say DOWN. When you elevate the flat right hand, you say HIGH, and when you hold it down near the ground, you say LOW.

All nations of earth have nodded the head for YES, and have shaken it for NO. If you will nod the right index finger beside the head, you say YES; and if, waist high, you simply turn the right hand over, you say NO. GOOD means "level with the heart," and, therefore, if you will swing the right flat hand out in a semi-circle from the heart towards the right you will say the word GOOD. BAD means "thrown away." Therefore, the motion of expelling something downwards with the right hand makes the word BAD. When you point your right thumb at your breast, you say ME. When you point your right index finger at the person you are with, you say YOU. When you point the same finger at someone else in the party, you say HIM or HER.

When you point the separated first and second fingers of the right hand out in front of the eyes, you say SEE or LOOK. When you pass the partly closed right hand downwards past the mouth, you say EAT or FOOD. When you elevate the cupped hand near the mouth, you say DRINK; and when, waist high, you make as though dipping a handful of something with cupped hand, you say WATER.

The flat hands passed alternately one beyond the other means WALK, and the same sign made more rapidly means RUN. To incline the head to right, towards the palms of both hands, means SLEEP, and to pass the flat hand slightly outwards from the chin means SPEAK or TALK. To cup the right hand behind the right ear means to LISTEN. The right index finger pointed upwards beside the face means MAN, or "the upright one"; and to pass the slightly hooked fingers of the right hand downwards over the hair means WOMAN, the basic conception being "she combs her hair." DAY means the opening up and NIGHT means the closing over, and the signs are simple and logical. (Pages 23 and 43.)

The thumb and index finger of right hand held in an incomplete circle and pointed at the sky means SUN. The same sign held flat near the waist means MONEY—a coin; the same sign with hand laid on the breast means a MEDAL, and if made against the left shoulder means a BRAND, while if tipped to the mouth like a cup it means WANT, or "I am thirsty for."

The fingers curved and pointing up, held near the ground, naturally means GRASS. The same sign, waist high, means BRUSH, while one hand held out in front at height of shoulder, fingers all pointing up, means a TREE, both hands held similarly means a FOREST. The same two hands held close to the breast means PEOPLE. One fist held up out in front of breast means a MOUNTAIN, while both fists means a chain of MOUNTAINS. Counting is indicated by the fingers, starting with the little finger of right hand.

As all articles and small qualifying adjectives are left entirely out—this being a skeleton language of ideas—a smaller vocabulary or code is used, the verbs and nouns being almost enough to convey the intelligence. Remember that 85% of all signs are made with the right hand. I believe the foregoing forty words will prove my opening statement that the language is entirely logical and elemental. I would suggest that you go over each of these words carefully, by checking them against the illustrations and their explanations in the book.

Splendid results in the study of sign have been attained by those who, as they go along, occasionally have a session with someone else who is interested in sign. If you are in scouting, you might start with a few available scouts or scout masters, otherwise with a few friends, and meet with them once a week for a definite session for an hour or two. You will be surprised at the way the interest and inquiry thus caused will increase your own knowledge, and how quickly the others will commence to bring out ideas that will greatly help you. After one or two meetings of the little club, require everybody to make up and bring to the next meeting some short phrases or sentences in the sign language. Working carefully along these lines you will undoubtedly be gratified at the advancement you will make.

TWO HUNDRED SIGNS IN MOST GENERAL USE

YES, NO, GOOD, BAD, COME, GO, WATER, EAT, DRINK, SEE, UP, DOWN, HIGH, LOW, ALL, ME, YOU, HIM, ME-ALL (Us or We), YOU-ALL (Ye), HIM-ALL (They), WALK, RUN, SLEEP, SMALL, FEW, BIG, BUY OR SELL, EXCHANGE, TRADE, STOP, WAIT, HOUSE, TEEPEE, TEN, COUNTING, QUESTION, WAGON, WANT, WRITING, READING, HUNT, SPEAK, LISTEN, LIE, LOOK, LITTLE TALK, SPEECH, TREE, NOW, FOREST, MAN, WOMAN, BOY, GIRL, WHITE MAN, NEGRO, INDIAN, HORSE, MEDICINE, CRAZY, WORK, YEAR, STEAL, FISH, SNAKE, SMELL, BREAKFAST, DINNER, SUP-PER, STRONG, BRAVE, HARD, PERHAPS, CONSIDER, MOTHER, FATHER, MOUNTAIN, MOUNTAINS, HEAP, CALLED, TIME, LONG TIME, BEFORE, AFTER, RIVER, NIGHT, DAY, COFFEE, LOVE, FOND, SUN, GOOD MORN-ING, GOOD EVENING, GAP (Mountain), MANY TIMES, TOWN OR CITY, EVERY LITTLE WHILE, PRISONER, WINTER OR YEAR, SIGN LANGUAGE, MORNING, NOON, EVENING, ABUSE, ACROSS, AFTERNOON, ALL GONE, AMONG, ANGRY, ARROW, ASTONISH, BEAR, BEAVER, BESIDE, WITH, TO-GETHER, BIRD, BLANKET, BOAT, BROOK, BROTHER, BUFFALO, CAMP, CANNOT, CHEYENNE, CHIEF, COLD, COLOR, COUNCIL, CROW, CRY, DANCE, DEER, DOG, DONE, EATEN ENOUGH, EFFORT, ELK, END, ESCAPE, EXPLAIN, FIRE, FLAG, GIVE, GIVE ME, GRASS, GROW, HALF, HALF BREED, HEART, HIDE, HOLE, HOW MANY, HUNGRY, JEALOUS, KEEP, KNIFE, KNOW, LAKE, LAUGH, LEAF, MANY, MUCH, MEDAL, MEMORY, METAL, MIRROR, MONEY, MOON, MOTOR CAR, MY OR MINE, POSSESSION, NEZ PERCE, OLD, OWL, PAWNEE, PEOPLE, PIPE, POOR, POOR IN FLESH, PORTRAIT, POWDER, PRAIRIE, PRIVATE TALK, PUSH, RAIN, RATTLESNAKE, RED, RING, ROPE, SHARP, SICK, SILENT, SING, SIOUX, SIT OR REMAIN, SNOW, SOLDIER, SPOTTED, STAR, STRIPED, SWIM, TASTE, THINK, THICK, THIN, TOBACCO, TOGETHER, UNDER-STAND, WAR, BEYOND.

AN INDIAN BLESSING

May the Great Mystery make sunrise in your heart: GREAT MYSTERY—WORK —SUNRISE—YOUR—HEART.

BOY SCOUT OATH EXPRESSED IN IDIOM

(The text of the oath is in lower case, the sign language version is in capitals.)

On my honor
OATH (God sees my hands, they are clean)

I will do my best
I—EFFORT—WORK

to do my duty to God
GOOD—WITH—GOD

and my country
WITH—MY—COUNTRY

and to obey the scout law.
OBEY—SCOUT—LAW,

To help other people at all times
I—WORK—WITH—ALL—PEOPLE—OFTEN

To keep myself physically strong,
I—KEEP—ME—STRONG

mentally awake,
MIND—ALIVE,

and morally straight.
HEART—GOOD.

EXAMPLES OF SENTENCE FORMATION

The following are a few examples of sentence formation, illustrating some of the Indian idiomatic construction and forms of sentence construction generally. Certain liberties of modern usage have been taken, such as the word "supper", which an old-time Indian would not have used. First we give the sentence with modern English construction, carrying the idea to be conveyed. Then in rotation are shown the signs to be made. Then in capitals we show the same thought, as interpreted in the idioms of sign language.

What is your name ? QUESTION - YOU - CALLED	*I am hungry and want something to eat.* I -HUNGRY - FOOD- WANT
Where is your home.? QUESTION-YOU-POSSESSION-HOUSE	*I am going home.* I - GO - HOUSE
How old are you ? QUESTION-HOW MANY-YOU-WINTER	*I feel very sad.* I-HEART-ON-THE-GROUND
The man became very old. MAN-MUCH-OLD-ARRIVE-THERE	*I have not seen you for a long time.* LONG TIME - SEE - NOT
Where do you live ? QUESTION - YOU - SIT	*I live here.* I - HOUSE - SIT
Have you had your supper ? QUESTION-YOU-EAT-SUNSET	*Where is your horse?* QUESTION-POSSESSION-HORSE

Turn to Pages **97, 98, 99** and **100** for Further Examples of Sentence Formation.

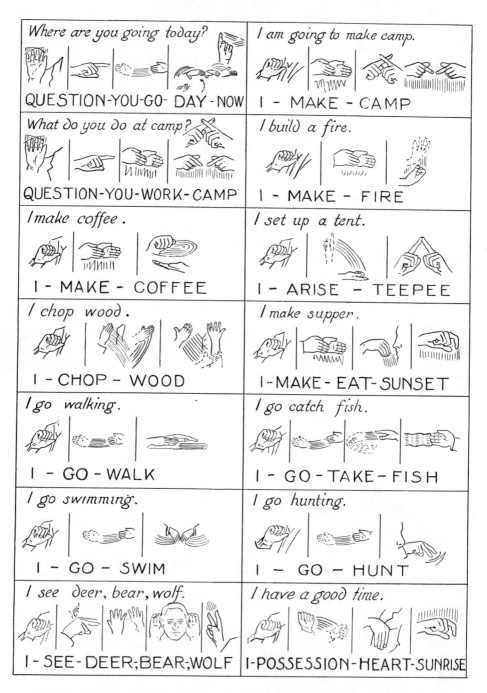

Where are you going today?	*I am going to make camp.*
QUESTION-YOU-GO- DAY -NOW	I - MAKE - CAMP
What do you do at camp?	*I build a fire.*
QUESTION-YOU-WORK-CAMP	I - MAKE - FIRE
I make coffee.	*I set up a tent.*
I - MAKE - COFFEE	I - ARISE - TEEPEE
I chop wood.	*I make supper.*
I - CHOP - WOOD	I-MAKE- EAT-SUNSET
I go walking.	*I go catch fish.*
I - GO - WALK	I - GO -TAKE- FISH
I go swimming.	*I go hunting.*
I - GO - SWIM	I - GO - HUNT
I see deer, bear, wolf.	*I have a good time.*
I - SEE- DEER; BEAR; WOLF	I-POSSESSION-HEART-SUNRISE

Turn to Pages **97, 98, 99** and **100** for Further Examples of Sentence Formation.

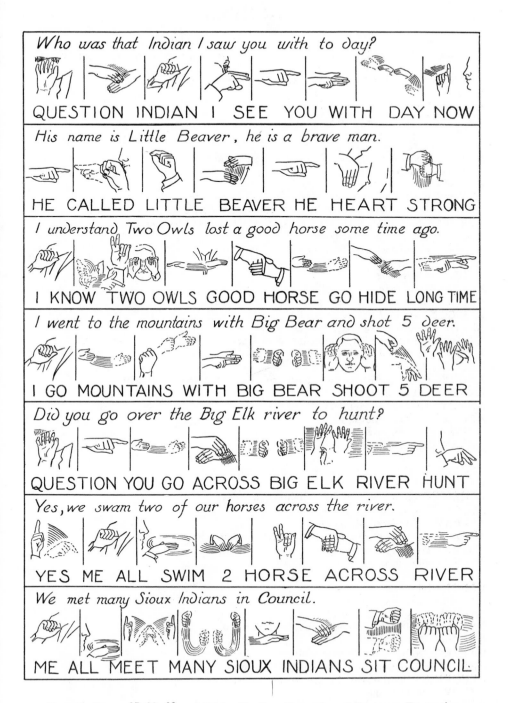

Who was that Indian I saw you with to day?

QUESTION INDIAN I SEE YOU WITH DAY NOW

His name is Little Beaver, he is a brave man.

HE CALLED LITTLE BEAVER HE HEART STRONG

I understand Two Owls lost a good horse some time ago.

I KNOW TWO OWLS GOOD HORSE GO HIDE LONG TIME

I went to the mountains with Big Bear and shot 5 deer.

I GO MOUNTAINS WITH BIG BEAR SHOOT 5 DEER

Did you go over the Big Elk river to hunt?

QUESTION YOU GO ACROSS BIG ELK RIVER HUNT

Yes, we swam two of our horses across the river.

YES ME ALL SWIM 2 HORSE ACROSS RIVER

We met many Sioux Indians in Council.

ME ALL MEET MANY SIOUX INDIANS SIT COUNCIL

Turn to Pages **97, 98, 99** and **100** for Further Examples of Sentence Formation.

SYNONYMS

Words of Similar Meaning to Basic Word Signs Contained in the Foregoing Work

ABANDONED—divorced, thrown away, displaced, deserted, forsaken.
ABOARD—sitting down, on top of.
ABUSE—Scold, ill-treat, upbraid, defame, detract.
ACCOMPANY—with, escort.
ACCOST—hail, salute, interrogate.
ACHE—physical pain, sick.
ACROSS—on the other side of, to cross, to pass over.
ADD—join, increase, put to.
ADVANCE—move, march.
ADVANCE GUARD—scout, before, ahead, foremost, to be in front.
AFRAID—shrink from, cowardly, suspicious, temerity, dread, nervous, fearful.
AFRAID OF NO ONE—brave, courageous, lion-hearted, fearless.
AFTER—since, by and by, later.
AID—assist, counsel, advice, help.
AIM, TO—point at.
ALIGHT—dismount.
ALIKE—same, even.
ALIVE—living, above ground, breathing.
ALL GONE—wiped out, consumed.
ALLIANCE—co-operation, confederacy, league.
AMBITIOUS—aspire after, long for, desire, crave.
AMONG—in the midst of, commingle.
ANCESTORS—progenitors, forefathers.
ANGRY—mad, rageful, savage, quarrelsome, ill-tempered, passionate.
ANNIHILATE—destroy.
ANNOY—disturb, agitate, trouble.
APPAREL—dress, clothing.
ARISE—start up, rise.
ARRANGE—plan, settle, adjust.
ARREST—seize.
ARRIVE HERE—reach here, come to a place, return.
ASCEND—climb.
ASHAMED—humbled, abashed, diffident, mortified.
ASTONISH—surprise, astound, awe.
ASTRAY—lost, deceived, wander.
ATTACK—assault, storm, fall upon, march against, advance against, fire at.
ATTEMPT—try, endeavor, strive.
AVOID—shun, pass by, elude.

BACON—fat, greasy.
BAD—mean, wrong, vile, detestable.
BARRACKS—soldiers' house.
BASHFUL—diffident, modest, youthful, shy, timid.
BASIN—buffalo-wallow.
BATTLE—volley firing, engagement.
BEAUTIFUL—good face, fine, handsome, pretty.
BEFORE (in time)—prior to, previously, anterior.
BELOW—beneath, under.
BET—wager, gamble, raffle, stake.
BEYOND—other side of.
BIG—great, wide, large, broad.

BITTER—unpalatable, unsavory, nasty, ill-flavored, sour.
BLESS YOU—thank, pray for, gratitude.
BOIL, TO—bubble, stew, cook.
BRAND, TO—mark, figure.
BRAVE—fearless, daring, bold, heroic.
BREAK—sunder, rend.
BRING—fetch.
BROAD—wide.
BROOK—small stream.
BURN—consume.
BURY—rite, sepulture.
BUY—purchase, procure, bargain.
BY AND BY—wait.

CACHE—conceal, hide away.
CALL—to name, known as, summon, cry out, invite.
CAMP—village, bivouac.
CANDID—sincere, honorable, frank, open, straightforward, undisguised.
CANNOT—impossible, will not do, beyond power.
CANYON—gorge, defile, chasm, gap.
CHARGE—assault, attack, onslaught, storm.
CHEAT—steal, fraud, deceit.
CHIEF—leader, headman, partisan, great, distinguished, renowned, famous.
CHILD—youth, progeny, issue, offspring.
CHOP—cut up, hew, divide.
CLOSE—near, compact, compress.
COLD—chill, frigid.
COLOR—tinge, hue, stain.
COME—approach, draw near.
COMMENCE—begin.
CONCEAL—cover, disguise, secrete, hide.
CORRAL—enclosure.
COUNCIL—meeting.
COUNT—numeration.
COWARD—poltroon, dastard.
CRAZY—mad, foolish, doting, flighty.
CROSS—sulky, ill-tempered.
CROSS (to)—ford, go over.
CRY—shed tears, desire, suffer.
CUNNING—subtle, sly, wily.

DECEIVE—lead astray.
DEFAME—slander, vilify.
DEFY—hatred, defiance, threaten.
DESTROY—waste, demolish.
DIE—expire, depart.
DISGUST—weary, dislike.
DISTANT—remote, far away.
DISTRIBUTE—give, divide.
DIVE—plunge.
DO—work, act, attend to.
DOCTOR—medicine-man, physician, priest, juggler.
DRESS—apparel, clothing.
DUMB—mute, silent, still.

EFFORT—trial, attempt, essay.
ELOPE—steal.

END—finish, close, stop.
ENEMY—foe.
EQUAL—same, even.
ESCAPE—elude, evade.
EXCHANGE—trade, barter, bargain, purchase, sell, dispose of, traffic.
EXTERMINATE—destroy, wipe out, eradicate, consume, sweep away, ravage, annihilate, extinguish.

FAME—renowned, celebrated.
FAST—swift, pass by.
FEAST—meal, repast.
FEW—compressed, close, crowded, near together.
FIGHT—skirmish, outbreak, battle, encounter.
FINISHED—ended, done.
FIX—settle, arrange, determine.
FOND—love, regard, liking.
FOOL—stupid, unwise, indiscreet, rash, silly.
FOREST—timber.
FORGET—lost.
FORT—barracks, post, garrison.
FRAGRANT—perfume, sweet-smelling, balmy.
FRIEND—companion, comrade, partner.

GALLOP—lope, canter, ride.
GAP—mountain pass, depression, defile, ravine.
GENEROUS—good-hearted, big-hearted, liberal, hospitable, noble.
GIVE—grant, bestow.
GLAD—heart good.
GLOOMY—sad.
GO—depart, leave.
GOD—mystery, medicine.
GRAVE—tomb, burial-place.
GREAT—wide, broad, large.

HAIL—ice, sleet.
HALT—stop, pause, stand still.
HANG (to)—suspend, pendent from.
HARD—difficult, firm, brave, unfeeling, inexorable.
HEAP—mound.
HEAR—attention.
HEAVY—weighty.
HELP—work with, assist, support.
HIDE (to)—secretly, privately, confidentially, lost, hidden away.
HOLD—detain, stop, limit, keep, retain.
HOMELY—bad face.
HUNT—search, look for.
HURRY—hasten, expedite.

IMPOSSIBLE—cannot.
IMPRISON—confine, lock up, bind.
INCREASE—augment.
INFERIOR—lower, behind, minor, subordinate, secondary.
INJURE—harm, hurt.
INTERROGATE—question, attract attention, ask, inquire, examine.

JEALOUS—envious.
JOKE—sport.
JOYOUS—glad, light-hearted.

KEEP—remember, hold on to, retain, guard, keep close, near.
KEEP QUIET—fear not, quiet down.
KNOW—understand, comprehend.

LARGE—great, capacious.
LAST—hindmost.
LIE—to mistake, invent, false, fabrication, fiction.
LIKE—same, even, similar, resemble.
LISTEN—hear, pay attention to.
LITTLE—minute.
LIVE—reside, dwell, exist.
LONG TIME—always.
LOOK—inspect, see, view, behold.
LOVE—esteem, liking, affection.

MANY—crowd, numerous, host, much.
MANY TIMES—often, repeat.
MEAN—small-hearted, stingy, selfish, miserly, penurious, shabby, greedy, rapacious, sordid, niggardly, low.
MEDICINE—mysterious, unknown, holiness, luck, vision, dream, fortune, chance.
MEDICINE-MAN—physician, prophet, juggler, dreamer, priest, magician, conjurer, seer, wizard, soothsayer, charmer.
MEET (to)—come together.
MEMORY—heart knows.
METAL—hard.
MIGRATE—move.
MINGLE—mix.
MISLEAD—deceive, lead astray.
MISS (to)—pass by.
MIX—blend, mingle.
MONEY—currency, cash, specie.
MOURN—grieve, cry for, lament, bewail.
MOVE—march.

NAME—called, cognomen.
NEAR—close by, contiguous, adjacent.
NOTIFY—tell, talk to.
NOW—present time, today.

OATH—Vow, to swear.
OBEY—listen to, pay attention to.
OLD—decrepit, aged, infirm.

PACK—place.
PARADE—troops.
PART—half.
PARTNER—brother, comrade.
PAYMASTER—money chief.
PEACE—truce.
PEAK—apex, summit, tip, crest.
PEOPLE—persons.
PERHAPS—to be possible, may be, doubtful, contingent.
PICKET—fasten.
PITY (to pity some one else)—sympathize, compassion, mercy, tender.
PLANT—to farm.
POOR—poverty, indigence, want, distress, destitute, pinched.
POOR—emaciated, weak, sinewless, wasted, leanness, puny, thin, starved, shrunk, skinny.
POSSESSION—ownership.

PRAIRIE—plains.
PRAY—supplicate, ask, beg, request, petition, demand, implore, entreat, address, impor-
tune.
PRIVATE—secretly, confidentially, in confidence, sacredly.
PROUD—vain, conceited.
PUSH—must, try.

QUARREL—scold, disputatious.
QUIET DOWN—subdue, silence.

RACE—to run, contest.
RAPIDS—swift-flowing waters.
RASH—foolish, brave, reckless, careless, adventurous.
REACH—arrive there.
RECOVER—restore.
REMAIN—stay.
REMEMBER—hold on to.
RESTRAIN—hold, confine, restrict.
RETREAT—flee from, escape.
RING—finger ornament.
RISING MAN—chief.
RIVER—stream.
ROAD—trail, way, route, pack, course.
ROCK—hard.
ROPE—cord, line.
RUN AGAINST—stumble.

SACRED—divine, holy, mysterious.
SAD—mournful, dejected, disappointed.
SADDLE (to)—to pack.
SAME—equal.
SAW—cut.
SCOLD—quarrel, find fault with.
SCOUT—advance-guard, picket, sentinel.
SCOUT (to)—search, watch, to trail, follow, hunt.
SEARCH—examine, scrutiny.
SEE—look.
SEIZE—grasp, imprison, find.
SEPARATE—diverge, branch off, to part, wander from.
SEW—fasten, stitch, tack.
SHARP—cutting edge, edge-tool.
SHAWL—wrap.
SHEEP—big-horn.
SHOOT—fire at, discharge.
SICK—ill, infirm, indisposed, suffer, diseased.
SILENT—dumb, close one's mouth, taciturn.
SINCE—after.
SIT—here, remain, stay, wait, rest.
SLEEP—rest, lie down.
SLOW—loiter, behindhand.
SMALL—short, low.
SMOOTH—even, level.
SOFT—miry.
SOUR—acid, tart.
SPEAK—talk, tell, say, relate.
SPY—scout, hunt, look.
STINGY—mean, penurious.

STOP—halt, wait.
STRAIGHT—true, direct.
STRONG—brave, vigorous, hearty, powerful.
SUPERIOR—greater, higher, above.
SURROUND—encircle, concentrate.

TAKE—appropriate, capture, catch, dispossess, confiscate, seize.
TALK—converse, speak, tell.
TASTE—flavor, sapidity.
TATTOO—mark.
TEEPEE—lodge, wigwam, tent.
THERE—at that place.
THINK—believe, opine, look upon, regard.
THREAD—line.
TIMBER—forest, trees.
TIRED—weary, fatigued, prostrated, faint, exhausted, overtasked.
TRACK—footprint.
TRADER—storekeeper, salesman.
TRAIL (to)—follow, search, look for, pursue, hunt.
TROUBLE—anxious, disturbed, restless, annoyed.
TRUE—straightforward, honest, reliable, candid.

UGLY—bad face, ill-favored, repulsive.
UNCERTAIN—doubtful, precarious.
UNDERSTAND—know.
UNLUCKY—unfortunate, bad.

VIGILANT—attention, heedful, watchful.
VILLAGE—camp, town.

WANT—wish, desire.
WATCH—time-piece.
WEAK—tired, feeble.
WHEN—at what time.
WHERE—at what place.
WHISKEY—liquor.
WHITES—people not indigenous to America.
WICKEY-UP—temporary shelter.
WIPED OUT—exterminated.
WISE—shrewd, sagacious, sharp, clever, keen, sound, long-headed.
WRAP—fold, pack up.

LOCATION OF EAST AND WEST IN SIGN LANGUAGE

In determining the points of the compass, the Indian associates his left side with the East, his right side with the West. This is explained by Garrick Mallery as follows:

"A gesture sign for sunrise, morning, is: Forefinger of right hand crooked in incomplete circle and pointed or extended to the left, then slightly elevated. In this connection it may be noted that when the gesture is carefully made in open country the pointing would generally be to the East, and the body turned so that its left would be in that direction. In a room in a city, or under circumstances where the points of the compass are not clearly understood, the left side supposes the East, and the gestures relating to sun, day, etc., are made with such reference."

PICTOGRAPHY AND IDEOGRAPHY OF THE
SIOUX AND OJIBWAY TRIBES OF
NORTH AMERICAN INDIANS

It is hoped that the following very brief treatise on the Pictographic writing of the American Indians will excite interest in that branch of study by all boys and girls and others who are interested in anthropological research.

The attentions and investigations of the author have been for a long time devoted to pictography and to sign language, two studies so closely connected that neither can be successfully pursued to the exclusion of the other.

The depiction of gesture and posture signs is considered in more than a general way, showing the intimate relation between a thought as expressed without words by signs, and a thought expressed without words by pictures, sometimes corresponding to those signs.

Picture writing is a mode of expressing thoughts, or noting facts, by marks. It is one distinctive form of thought writing without reference to sound—gesture language being the earlier form. Picture writing should be studied as a phase in the evolution of human culture.

While not specifically reported in history it is thought from general evidence that picture writing preceded and generated the graphic systems of Egypt, Assyria and China, but in North America its use is still current. It can be studied here without inference or hypothesis, in actual existence, as applied to records and communications. In this connection it should be noted that picture writing is found in sustained vigor on this continent—the same continent where sign language has prevailed and has continued in active operation to an extent historically unknown in other parts of the world.

Petroglyphs, or rock carvings, are most frequently found in those parts of the world which are still, or recently have been, inhabited by savage or barbarian tribes, who, when questioned about the authorship of rock drawings, generally attributed them to supernatural beings. Man has invariably attributed to supernatural action whatever he did not understand.

Authorities are disagreed as to whether sign language, which is closely connected with picture writing, preceded articulate speech. It is sufficient to admit the undoubted antiquity of thought writing in both its forms.

Investigation has proven the interesting psychologic fact that primitive or at least very ancient man made the same figures in widely separated regions, though it is not established that the same figures had a common significance. The modern specimens of picture writing shown on skins, bark and pottery, are far more readily interpreted than those on rocks, and have already afforded verification as to points of history, religion, customs and other details. American pictographs are not to be regarded as mere curiosities, but rather as representing the only intellectual remains of the early inhabitants, and bearing significantly upon the evolution of the human mind.

A knowledge of Indian customs, costumes, histories and traditions is, of course, essential to the understanding of their drawings. It is probable that many were intended to commemorate events which to their authors were of moment, but would be of little importance as history.

Though the picture writings do not, and probably never will, disclose the kind of information hoped for by some enthusiasts, they surely are valuable in marking the steps in one period of human evolution, and in presenting evidence of man's early practices.

The word signs presented in this work are of both ancient and modern American origin, and found either as petroglyphs, or rock carvings; petrographs, or rock writings; or as pictographs or writings on skins, bark, pottery, etc.

Petroglyphs and pictographs have been found and catalogued from the pyramids of Egypt to India, from Australia to Brazil, from Japan to Scotland, and in Mexico, and in many cases have handed down important traditional history of the times and peoples represented.

More distinctive examples of evolution in ideography and in other details of picture writing are found still extant among the Dakota (or Sioux) Indians than among any other North American tribes.

The pictographic symbols used in this codification are taken from some of the most important known pictographs of the North American Indians. The classification and correlation of the matter collected has required more effort than is apparent, because the sources of information are so meager.

The more modern forms are explained by Indians who have kept up the pictographic practice, and these frequently throw light upon the more ancient.

This simple work is prepared for those men who desire brief, preliminary information on the subject, and does not assume to be anything further than that. During a series of lectures given by the author on sign language and pictography he was greatly impressed with the general lack of any knowledge on the subject, but most of all with the deep and kindly interest displayed by thousands of people in picture writing, which suggested the advisability of including a brief outline of some of the most generally used symbols.

Again, it is done in the hope that it will prove of interest and value to the youth of the United States, and develop in them an earnest desire for further study and research along this line.

Many of the pictographs herein contained are from the 10th annual report of the Bureau of American Ethnology, by Lieut.-Col. Garrick Mallery, 1888, and from historical information of the Bureau of Indian Affairs, prepared by Henry R. Schoolcraft, 1851, and from other similar authoritative sources.

THE AUTHOR.

Longfellow was deeply interested in pictography, and gave the best and briefest description of nine symbols that has ever been compiled. It is given in the following verse from Hiawatha.

> "For the earth he drew a straight line,
> For the sky a bow above it;
> White the space between for day-time,
> Filled with little stars for night-time;
> On the left a point for sunrise,
> On the right a point for sunset,
> On the top a point for noontide,
> And for rain and cloudy weather
> Waving lines descending from it."

There is no doubt but that gesture language has had an immense use and value in the past. The question now arises as to whether or not its usefulness is gone. Has mankind so far advanced that he can entirely disregard the refinements of primitive man? As an argument to the contrary we might offer the following:

When the obelisk of Luxor was installed in Paris, and the best minds of that modern nation were called on to determine in what manner they should inscribe the record of the Paris of today, did they do it in the current French language? Did they do it in Greek or Latin? No, they inscribed it in primitive pictography, so that future generations countless thousands of years from now, when the French and Greek and Latin languages are gone and forgotten, can readily read the inscriptions made at this time.

American	Antelope	Arrows	Bad	Bear alive
Bear dead	Bear sad heart	Bear glad heart	Beaver	Beaver in his house
Beaver Tail	Big Voice	Bird Tracks	Black Deer	Blanket
Headless Bodies	Bow and Arrow	Boy	Brothers	Buffalo
White Buffalo	Indian Camp	Canoe	Canoe and warriors	Cheyenne
Cloud	Cold and Snow	Come or Call for	Plenty Corn	Whooping Cough
Big Crow	White Crow	Calumet Dance	Council	Crane
Dakota or Sioux	Dakotas and Cheyennes Make Peace	Day	Death	Deer Tracks

Deer, Moose	Direction	Discovery	Dog	Duck
Eagle	Eagle Tail	Eat	Encampment	Evening
Famine	Fear	Fear	Fire	Camp Fire
Fish	Peace Flag	Grave Flag	Plenty Food	Fort
Fox	Black Fox	Froze to Death	Girl	Goods
Goose	Grasp	Gun	White Hawk	Heart
Hard	Hear	Hit	Horse	Spotted Horse
Horse Tracks	Hungry	Stole Horses	Fast Horse	Ropes Horses

Hunt	Island	Knife	Lake	Wild Horse
Lariat	Leggings	Life	Lightning	Long Hair
Lynx	Man on horse back	Man holding gun	Man	Man
Tall white man	Wise Man	Man Grieves	Man holding bow	Man disabled
Mandan	Measles	Many, cache, heap.	Medicine Man	Medicine Teepee
Medicine Lodge	Medicine Man	Medicine Man	Plenty Meat	Moon, night sun
Morning, sunrise	Moose	Mountain	Negation	Night
Night	Three Nights	Noon	Omaha Indian	Old

Making Peace	Peace Pipe	Pipe	Pipe	Thunder Pipe
Medicinal Plants	Porcupine	Power	Prisoners	Jack Rabbit
Rain and Cloudy	Ran	Rattlesnake	Rest	River
River Fight	River Flood	Road	See	Sea
Shell	Mountain Goat	Sick	Sky	Smallpox
Snake	Deep Snow	Deep Snow	Sociability	Soldier
Spotted Face	Spirit	Spirits Above	Bad Spirit Medicine	Great Spirit Everywhere
Speaks	Storm and Windy	It Struck	Starvation	Stars

Sunrise	Sunset	Sun	Sun	Swallow
Talk	Talk together	Teepee (Man Reached)	Teepee	Thirty
Thunder bird	Tree	Same Tribe	Tracks	Trade
Treaty	Tomahawk	Top Man	Three Years	Wading Birds
Walked passed	War Bonnet	Raising War Party	War	War
Water Carrier	Calling for Rain	Weather Clear	Weather Stormy	Whirlwind
Horse (White Man's)	White Beaver	White Hawk	White Man	Whooping Cough
Wind	Wolf	Woman	Woman	Winter

Cactus	Canyon	Christian	Corn	Dead
Drum and Stick	Drumstick	Earth Lodge	Geese	Grass
Stone Hammer	I did it	Hidden, Obscure	House	I or Me
Inspired	Meteor	Moon (new hung)	Moon (reached half)	Moon (full)
Mouse	Old	Otter	Prayer	Prisoner
Shining, Bright	Singing	Snow	Strong	Rising Sun
Supplication	Talk (intense)	Thunder Bird	Travois	Old Tree
Turkey	Turtle	Walk	War	Woods

Holds the Arrows   Little Dog   High Eagle   Caught the Enemy

Spotted Elk   Two Eagles   Chief Standing Bear   Drags the Rope

Big Chief   Swimming Swan   Loud Talker   Takes Prisoner

The above twelve pictographs represent proper names of Indians.

Little Elk _ size is indicated by the relative proportion.

Food was scarce and they had to live on acorns Cloud Shield's winter count for year 1787

"Your own tongue kill you". Bitter words denoted by an arrow pointed towards himself.

Two ways of expressing time. A circle represents one year, each device represents 3 years.

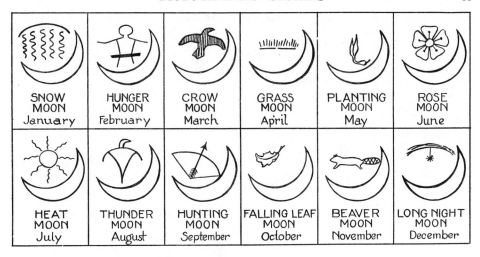

SNOW MOON January	HUNGER MOON February	CROW MOON March	GRASS MOON April	PLANTING MOON May	ROSE MOON June
HEAT MOON July	THUNDER MOON August	HUNTING MOON September	FALLING LEAF MOON October	BEAVER MOON November	LONG NIGHT MOON December

A PICTOGRAPHIC STORY FOR OUR YOUNG FRIENDS

Here is a story that might be entitled, "Sioux Bros., Arrow Makers." It is told in the pictography of the Sioux and Ojibways.

To read this story, which is written on a hide, the reader begins in the center and reads to the left, following the circular course to the end.

This story begins with the two men, who by virtue of the connecting line between them, are brothers. Followed by an Indian and an arrow, they are arrow makers.

Next comes a series of lines illustrating tracks; so they "make tracks," or "go" to those three peaks which are obviously mountains. The head with the line going from the eye indicates that they are looking. Looking for what? For arrow head, or by implication, for material with which to make arrow heads. The story so far, therefore, would read:

"Two brothers, Indian arrow makers, went to the mountains to look for material for arrows."

It is implied that they found the needed rock, for the story goes on to say they built a fire—those three crossed sticks with flame about them, on the mountain to heat the rock. Then the figure of the man with the pail in his hand indicates that they poured water on the rock.

The next symbol is a "cache"—a mound or hiding place in which many things are kept. This symbol is used to indicate "many." On heating the rock it broke up so they could get at the unweathered or underlying flint. The story therefore continues:

"They found a flint outcrop, heated the rock, poured water on it and thereby removed the weathered outer layer. They then obtained many pieces of good flint, which they made into arrowheads."

"They found a flint-rock, lit a big fire, heated the rock, carried water and poured it on the rock, and it burst into many pieces suitable for arrowmaking."

Then comes the sign indicating "to see," with the line pointing at a tree (from which they could obtain wood for arrows). Then follows an arrow pointing to an eagle, indicating that they then shot an eagle, which they killed—for the eagle is repeated, lying on its side. In others words, "They shot and killed an eagle to obtain feathers for the arrows."

After this, they "make tracks" again, and come to a lake, in which they catch a fish. The figure of the man with his hand to his mouth tells that they ate the fish. Again they "make tracks" until they come to their home, or teepee. Freely translated, "They started for home and came to a lake where they caught a fish, and, after eating it, they went on until they reached home."

Next we see two Indians, one of them a chief, as indicated by the feather in his hair, surrounded by a lot of lines. These lines are other Indians sitting in a circle, and the whole is the picture of a council. The next pictures tell the reason for the council; a Cheyenne (Cheyennes are "finger choppers") with a lariat, a horse and a number of horse hoofs, indicates that a Cheyenne had stolen some of their horses.

Three lines followed by a sun indicates that the council lasted three days, after which they joined hands—made peace—and smoked the pipe of peace. The story therefore concludes:

"They found a council in session on account of trouble with the Cheyennes, due to the fact that a Cheyenne had stolen some of their horses. The council was held for three days, and resulted in their making peace with the Cheyennes, after which they smoked the pipe of peace and everybody was happy."

The characters in these pictographic stories are arranged in a spiral formation, the course of the spiral being from right to left, starting from right center and reading backwards. This form is used in Lone Dogs' Winter Count and certain other famous Sioux documents.

Interpretation of Above Pictographic Story

An Indian trader by the name of Little Crow went on a journey. He traveled for three nights until he came to a river. The reason he traveled at night was because he was in enemy country. At the river he secured a canoe, camped there that evening, and at sunrise the next morning started down the river and traveled two suns (days). He now traveled in daytime, because he was in friendly territory. He was an Indian trader in shells, which were used for wampum and ornamentation. At the end of the fifth day's travel he reached the village where the shells were obtainable. He rested there for three days in conference with the chief, and as a result he traded for a large amount of shells, and at sunrise on the fourth day he loaded his canoe and started down the river and traveled for two days. On the second day a storm came up, with rain and lightning. He saw the lightning strike a tree and set it afire. As a result of the storm he became sick, so he searched and found some medicinal plants and waited there a couple of days until he felt better. He then traveled at night and hid away in the day time. He knew that the country abounded in game because he heard foxes and wolves. He finally reached home, though some days late. Twenty braves of the tribe came out to meet him, including their chief, Standing Bear. Their hearts were glad as a result of his safe and successful trip, and they all had a very sociable time.

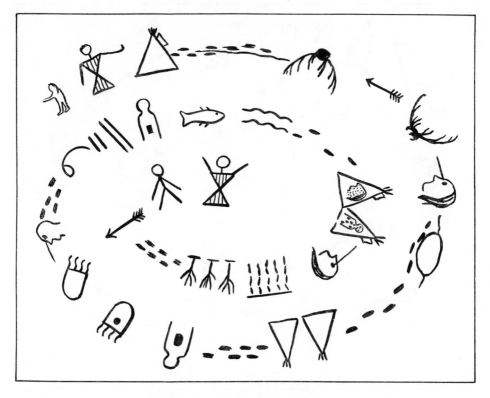

Interpretation of Above Pictographic Story

An Indian and his wife had a quarrel; he wanted to go hunting and she did not want him to go. He gave the sign of negation, would not do what she wanted, and he took his bow and arrows and started into the forest. A snow storm came upon him and he looked for shelter. He saw two teepees, went over to them, but found that they contained two people who were sick, in one teepee a boy with the measles, in the other teepee a man with the smallpox. He ran away as fast as he could and shortly came to a river. He saw some fish in the river, so he caught a fish, ate it, and rested there for two days. After that he started out again and saw a bear. He shot and killed the bear and had quite a feast. Then he started on again and saw an Indian village, but as they proved to be enemies he ran away until he came to a little lake. While walking around the lake he saw a deer. He shot and killed it and dragged it home to his teepee, to his wife and his little boy.

Death of an animal is indicated by the animal being shown in an inverted position, viz. upside down.

In case of a deer being shown by a set of deer horns, reverse the horns to represent death. Where a bear is shown by the bear's paw, reverse the paw with claws up to represent death.

In case of a person, have animal representing family totem shown upside down to represent death.

Interpretation of Above Pictographic Story

Two brothers, one of them a chief, by the names of Spotted Elk and White Beaver, together with their tribe, experienced a severe winter of deep snow and stormy weather, and three members of the same tribe froze to death. They suffered a famine and their wives were very hungry and their little girl, two years old, had the whooping cough. They sent for the Medicine Man but he did no good and the little girl died. Everybody grieved greatly. Then the top man of the tribe had a conference with the wise man of the village who told them that the sun would soon come out, the weather would get warm, the rivers would run and the buffalo would come near to their camp and they would have plenty of food.

What he said came true and in three days the lookout on the hill signaled that he had discovered the buffalo. They secured a large quantity of meat which they cured on the drying poles and were quite happy, but they did not forget to place a flag of sorrow on the little girl's grave.

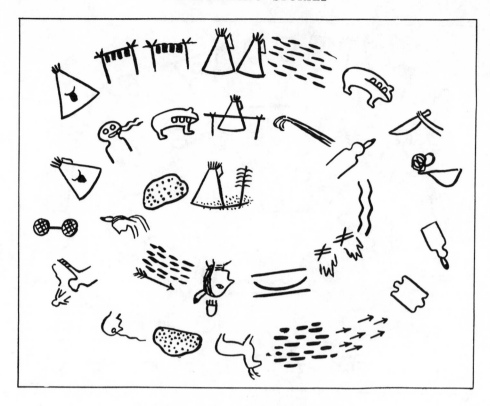

Interpretation of Above Pictographic Story

During the great famine of 1787 the Indians were forced, for a time, to live on acorns, so a great many Sioux, in desperation, organized a big hunt and started out headed by their Chief, White Bear. The weather was clear, fine hunting weather. The first night out they camped by a river. The Chief was filled by fear of famine to his tribe, and his heart was very sad. He therefore called his council together and told them they must go to the Medicine Lodge and make Hunting Medicine for two days and nights. At the end of that time a friendly Cheyenne Indian by the name of Drags-the-Rope came into camp and said that he had seen a great many antelope. They believed him and a large party went out on the hunt and secured a large amount of antelope meat. The Chief, however, was disabled. A wild horse was dragging a rope which caught him, but he drew his knife and cut the rope and was saved, and all the tribe was happy. They went back to the village and took the antelope meat along. Then they all went to the Medicine Lodge and gave thanks for the successful hunt.

PICTOGRAPHIC CORRESPONDENCE OF TODAY

Some time ago Keesakawasis, Chief Day Child, of the Rocky Boy Tribe of Chippewa Indians, located at Rocky Boy, Montana, through his talented secretary Sitting Eagle, wrote to the author regarding his endeavors to trace certain records with reference to the lost tribe of Chippewas of which his people are descendants. As Keesakawasis himself can neither speak nor write English, and as the writer has no knowledge of Chippewa, it became necessary for us to communicate by means of Indian pictography, which proved to be quite satisfactory. The first letter and its interpretation follows:—

In the upper left hand corner is the date, Feb. 15, indicated as the 15th day of the hunger moon. Then comes the chief's name; the Indian with the feather is the chief, and the next two signs are "day" and "child". A careful translation of the letter is as follows:

"I see your talking leaf and my heart is big for you. I pray the great mystery that I may travel to your teepee, and that we may have a long talk together as brothers. (The two figures at the right of the teepee are having the long talk the chief designated by his symbol, Tomkins by the hat which makes him a white man. The line joining them at the bottom makes them brothers.) The Indian sky is everywhere overcast with clouds. The old Indian trail was good. The Chief and his white brother will travel the ancient path together toward the light. I look eagerly for your pictured message of reply.

(Signed)   SUNKA WAKAN WAHTOGLA".

Keesakawasis was delighted to find that he had a white brother to whom he could write his ancient pictorial language. He is over 70 years old but still in the full possession of his faculties, and actively heads the tribe of which he is a member. To his Sioux brothers William Tomkins has been known for many years as Sunka Wakan Wahtogla, or Wild Horse. The text of the Chief's letter of reply and its interpretation follows:

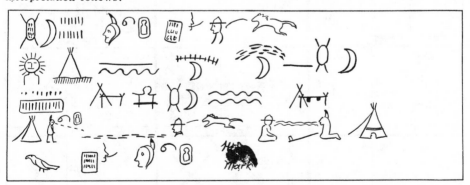

"In the 14th day of the Frog Moon, Day Child writes to his friend Wild Horse, who is a wise man. The winter was cold and stormy from the Frost Moon. The Fog Moon there was much snow and cold, and in our teepees we were hungry. Now it is the Frog Moon and the river runs and we again have a little meat. I look for the coming of my friend Wild Horse when we can sit in my teepee, talk and smoke much kinni kinnick. Sitting Eagle helps me write. Your friend DAY CHILD."

Below	Brothers	Come
Day	Deer	Eat
Fear	Grass	Hear
Heart	Hungry	Lightning
Many –(heap)	Moon	Mountain
Old	Peace	Rain
See	Snake	Sun
Talk	Trade	Tree

ancient form (E ... W)

CO-RELATING SIGN LANGUAGE AND PICTOGRAPHY

All Indian language is highly figurative and poetical compared to ours, resembling the Chinese in its idiomatic construction, but I know of nothing that gives so complete an insight into the peculiarities of Indian thought and expression as does a thorough study of their universal sign language.

Whatever form of picture writing Indians adopt, it must necessarily be based upon the same general sequence of thought as their spoken or gestured language, and in this way alone sign language becomes of prime importance in all pictographic study.

Whether there is any direct connection between the gestured and pictured signs themselves is a question that has been largely ignored, the general presumption probably being that there is little if any relation between the two. With the exception of Garrick Mallery's monograph very little if any effort seems to have been made to correlate the Indian Sign Language and Indian Pictography. Perhaps the question seems too remote to merit serious consideration. But if something could be done to prove such a connection it would be of the greatest importance in view of the fact that so little is known of pre-Columbian America.

It is evident that the Indian pictographs and the more ancient rock carvings are the most important basis we have for a comparison of the life and habits of past races of early man in America with the Indians of today.

Some of the pictographic symbols which have been used for long periods of time by the Sioux and Ojibway tribes seem to indicate that further research may show a definite relationship between the gestured and written signs.

A few of the most striking examples supporting this assumption are shown on page 90.

The above is offered for the consideration of our readers, and we hope may point the way to still more important findings in this direction.

"In primitive picture-writing, each sign meant a whole sentence and even more—the image of a situation or of an incident being given as a whole; this developed into an ideographic writing of each word by itself; this system was succeeded by syllabic methods, which had in their turn to give place to alphabetic writing, in which each letter stands for, or is supposed to stand for, one sound."

JESPERSEN, the Danish philologist.

"Gesture language stands on the threshold of picture and sign writing, as it consists chiefly of successive and transient delineations of objects, phenomena and symbols."

PROF. TERRIEN DE LACOUPERIE.

"Spoken sounds preceded written figures, and, before the invention of written symbols, dealings by means of knotted cords came into existence. These were followed by cutting notches on wooden materials, WHICH GAVE WAY, IN TURN, TO FIGURES REPRESENTING NATURAL OBJECTS, AND FORMS INDICATIVE OF ACTIONS, states or relations, cut out into lines to serve as counterparts of the spoken names of the same objects, actions, states or relations. With these came graving knives, and tablets for graving upon, and this was writing, the whole object of which was to make speech visible."   TIA TUNG, 1300 A. D.

"Ideographic writing directs the mind of the reader by means of a picture or a symbol directly to the idea existing in the mind of the one who uses it, while alphabetic or literal writing is simply the written expression of the sound, and only indirectly expresses the idea."   PROF. C. J. RYAN, Theosophical University, San Diego.

"There is one great broad line that divides the nations and civilizations of the earth, past and present, in all their arts of expression. We may call it that of the ideographic or general, as against the literal or definite. It controls the inner form of language and of languages; it manifests in the passage of thought from man to man; it determines whether the writing of the people shall be hieroglyphic or alphabetic."

PROF. WILLIAM GATES, Peabody Institute.

SMOKE SIGNALS

The author has been asked many times to include a code of smoke signals in this book, for the benefit of the Boy Scouts and others. Smoke signals were not a standardized code as in the sign language. Inasmuch as they aimed to transmit secret knowledge, most or many of the signs were devised privately and to suit a particular purpose or the caprice of the transmitter.

As the signals were visible to all, unless they had a secretly understood significance they would be conveying the information alike to friend and enemy. There were, however, certain more or less recognized abstract smoke signals, of which the following are a few. One puff meant ATTENTION. Two puffs meant ALL'S WELL. Three puffs of smoke, or three fires in a row. signifies DANGER, TROUBLE OR A CALL FOR HELP.

An interesting diversion can be had by a party of Boy Scouts or others who will first pre-arrange their code of signals, then some members of the party go to an adjacent high hill or mountain, where they build a fire for the purpose on a visible point. After bringing the small fire to a blaze, a smoke fire is created by adding some handfuls of grass or with some green branches which may have been carried up for the purpose. Apart from the fire the most necessary adjunct is a blanket or tarp' to control the smoke, which when the fire is smoking well is liberated in a series of puffs, which convey the message.

At this point we would like to emphasize the importance of three signals of any kind as indicating danger or a call for help. If any boy is ever in serious trouble where he needs to call for help, three shouts, three whistles, three shots from a gun, three smoke signals, three fires in a row at night in a place where they might be visible, all should be interpreted to convey the message that a person is in danger or requires assistance.

It should be impressed upon all boys that the number three, whether in shots, fires, whistles or smokes, is the distress signal of Boy Scouts and of all woodsmen, plainsmen, and outdoor people generally. The importance of this signal cannot be overestimated. It should always be borne in mind that under no circumstances should this signal ever be given except in case of actual necessity, and never in a joking or foolish manner.

HISTORY OF SIGN LANGUAGE

SOME RESEARCH WITH REFERENCE TO THE ORIGIN AND WIDE DISSEMINATION OF INDIAN SIGN LANGUAGE IN NORTH AMERICA.

Much deserved credit is due the Plains Indians for having developed and perpetuated the Indian sign language. So much credit has been given them in this regard that the language has been commonly known as the sign language of the Plains Indians, by which title, in keeping with general usage, it is referred to in the pages of this work. Inasmuch, however, as investigation has served to indicate that the language has other and more remote origin, the author has made something of a hobby of research along this line and is pleased to freely offer his findings, for such conclusion as more capable students may determine.

Some authorities contend that because gesture is practically unknown among the present Indians of the Southwest, that it was never known in that region. This alone has been enough to stimulate the author to research along this line, if only in a spirit of fairness, and we offer our findings for the consideration of the jury of those who shall peruse these pages.

Every record of the landing of Columbus tells of how they communicated with the Indians by signs. The records of all early explorers have information of this nature. It is contended that these general statements are true of all parts of the world, therefore the task devolves of proving by research and deduction that the North American signs comprised a more perfect language and were the forerunner of the sign language contained herein. Let us take for example the story of the landing of Cabrillo in San Diego Bay in September, 1542. A free translation of the visit, contained in the U. S. Geographic Report of 1879, reads as follows:

"And the following day, in the morning, there came to the ship three large Indians, and by signs they said that there were traveling in the interior men like us, with beards. and clothes and armed like those of the ships, and they made signs that they carried cross-bows and swords, and made gestures with the right arm as if they were throwing lances, and went running in a posture as if riding on horseback, and made signs that they killed many of the native Indians, and that for this they were afraid. This people are well disposed and advanced; they go covered with the skins of animals."

In Coronado's Journal, 1540, speaking of the Tonkawa, or Comanche, tribes that inhabited the district now known as Western Texas, he states:

"That they were very intelligent is evident from the fact that although they conversed by means of signs, they made themselves understood so well that there was no need of an interpreter." . . . "They are kind people and not cruel, they are faithful, they are able to make themselves very well understood by means of signs."

Garrick Mallery, of the Smithsonian Institute, said in 1879 that though some suggest a Spanish origin of sign, there is ample evidence that the Spaniards met signs in their early explorations north of and in the northern parts of Mexico, and availed themselves of them, but did not invent them. He said it is also believed by some authorities that the elaborate system of picture writing of Mexico was founded on gesture signs.

Dr. Wm. H. Corbusier, Surgeon U. S. Army, a deep student of Indian affairs, said in 1878:

"The traditions of the Indians point towards the South as the direction from which the sign language came." "The Comanches acquired it in Mexico." "The Plains Indians did not invent it."

Dr. Francis H. Atkins, Surgeon U. S. Army, in his early writings over fifty years ago, alludes to the effect of the Spanish, or rather the "lingua Mexicana," upon all the Southern tribes as well as upon some of those to the North, by which "Recourse to signs is now rendered less necessary."

Rev. J. O. Dorsey contended fifty years ago that the Poncas in Indian Territory never saw sign language until they were sent south to that district.

Cabeça de Vaca in 1528 said that the Indians of Tampa Bay were active in the use of signs, and in his journeying for eight subsequent years through Texas and Mexico, remarked that he passed through many dissimilar tongues, but that he questioned and received the answers of the Indians by signs "Just as if they spoke our language and we theirs."

Ruxton, in his "Adventures in Mexico and the Rocky Mountains," (New York, 1848,) sums up his experiences with regard to the southwestern tribes so well as to require quotation.

"The language of signs is so perfectly understood in the Western country, and the Indians themselves are such admirable sign talkers, that, after a little use, no difficulty whatever exists in carrying on a conversation by such a channel; and there are few mountain men who are at a loss in thoroughly understanding and making themselves intelligible by signs alone, although they neither speak or understand a word of the Indian tongue."

Mr. Ben Clark, the skillful interpreter at Fort Reno, stated:

"The Cheyennes think the sign language originated with the Kiowas, who brought it from Mexico."

Col. Richard I. Dodge, U. S. Army, considered in 1875, through an experience of over 30 studious years among the American Indians, to be an authority, said:

"The Plains Indians believe that the sign language was invented by the Kiowas." (who lived to the Southward.) "It is certain that the Kiowas are more universally proficient than any other Plains tribe."

In Bossu's "Travels through that part of North America formerly called Louisiana," (Forster's translation, London, 1771,) an account is given of a party who remained with them two years and "Conversed in their pantomimes with them."

In the report of Fremont's expedition of 1844 special and repeated allusion is made to the expertness of the Piutes in signs, also regarding a band of Indians near the summit of the Sierra Nevada, and a band of "Digger" Indians encountered on a tributary of the Rio Virgen who were likewise well versed in signs.

Ernest Thompson Seton says that he found sign language, many years ago, to be a daily necessity when traveling among the natives of New Mexico, also that in Western Manitoba and Montana he found it used among the various Indian tribes as a common language.

Dr. E. B. Tyler, the eminent authority who wrote "Researches into the early history of mankind," after a lifetime of study stated that "The same signs serve as a medium of converse from Hudson Bay to the Gulf of Mexico."

Many of the Indians, in a variety of tribes, have stated that in former times the sign language was the one common and universal means of communication between all the tribes of American Indians who spoke different vocal languages. As he expressed it, "All the old people in all the tribes used it."

Little Raven, the former head chief of the Southern Arapahoes, said in regard to the use of gestures: "I have met Comanches, Kiowas, Apaches, Caddos, Gros Ventres, Snakes, Crows, Pawnees, Osages, Arickarees, Nez Percés, Cherokees, Choctaws, Chickasaws, Sacs and Foxes, Pottawattomies, and other tribes whose vocal languages, like those of the tribes named, we did not understand, but we communicated freely in sign language."

"The summer after President Lincoln was killed we had a grand gathering of all the tribes to the east and south of us. Twenty-five different tribes met near old Fort Abercrombie on the Wichita River. The Caddos had a different sign for horse, and also for moving, but the rest were made the same by all the tribes."

Chief Joseph of the Nez Percés said that his tribe learned the language from the

Blackfeet, some 80 years earlier, and yet it is a well-known fact that these Indians used gesture speech long before that time.

Nichelle, chief of the Pend d'Oreilles, said: "All the tribes talk in signs when they meet if they cannot understand each other's vocal language. The Blackfeet, Crows, Flat-heads, Kootenays, Peleuses, Cayuses, Pend d'Oreilles, Coeur d'Alenes, Spokanes, Nez Percés, Yakimas and others all make the same signs.

"When I was a boy my grandfather told me that a long time ago when two tribes met that did not speak the same vocal language, they always talked in signs."

In the record of Major Long's expedition, of which he wrote in 1822, it tells how on his way down the Mississippi a number of strange Indians came into his camp, and Mr. Nolin, who was present, addressed them in such of the languages as he was ac-quainted with and was not understood. He then conversed by certain signs. These were fully understood by the Indians and were answered in like manner. Directly a conver-sation ensued in which not a word was spoken. "This," said Nolin, "is a universal lan-guage common to the Western Tribes."

Dr. W. Matthews and Dr. W. C. Bateler, who made comparisons of the signs re-ported by the Prince of Wied in 1832, proved the remarkable degree of permanency of the signs, most of which have persisted unchanged in their essentials.

In the report of Major Long's expedition of 1819 among a number of scattered In-dian tribes it states that being ignorant of each other's languages, "many of them when they met would communicate by means of signs, without difficulty or interruption."

Michaelius, writing in 1628, says of the Algonquins on or near the Hudson River: "For purposes of trading as much was done by signs with the thumb and fingers as by speaking."

There is some recorded testimony and evidence of extensive early use of gesture signs by several tribes of Iroquoian and Algonkian families, although their advanced social condition worked against its continuance. The gradual decadence of signs used by our Indians in general arose from their general acquaintance with the English language.

The Rev. Edward Jacker, in 1878, contributed to the Bureau of American Ethnology valuable information upon the use of gesture language in earlier times by the Ojibways of Lake Superior.

From remoter parts of North America we learn, prior to 1879, from Mr. J. W. Powell, Indian Superintendent, of the use of sign language among the Kutine; and from Mr. James Lenihan, Indian Agent to the Selish, of their using signs; both tribes of British Columbia.

The pueblo of Taos is, of all the pueblos, the farthest east and north, and has at all times been the connecting link between the Plains Indians and the Desert Indians. Intermarriage was frequent, and as a result the sign language, if it had not been there already, would naturally have been disseminated through the entire Southwest.

Two widely separated historic incidents illustrate the use to which natural sign language had been put when white men first met Indians. When Captain John Smith and some of his followers had their first conference with Indians, after a skirmish in which the Indians had been repulsed with the loss of their idol, the record says:

Captain John Smith, stepping forward, stood face to face with the dark-skinned messenger, and BY DINT OF MANY GESTURES made himself understood.

This was the message he made the Indians understand "by dint of gestures:"

"If you will send six unarmed men to load my boat with provisions, I will return your idol and give you beads and copper, and will be your friend. Say this to your com-rades while we await their answer."

On the western side of the continent, up in Oregon, French traders met the Indians many years later. Telling of the first meeting, the chief of the Nez Percés said: "Our people could not talk with these white-faced men, but they used signs, which all people understand."

GENERAL USE OF IDIOMS

While the idiom is held in small esteem by some schoolmasters and old-fashioned grammarians, good writers in general admire and use it, for it is, in truth, "the life and spirit of language."

Throughout this work various examples are shown of seemingly peculiar idiomatic construction. This is no different from the English language, which is just as idiomatic in its construction and use. The writer has found over 2100 idioms in the English language, some of which follow:

At beck and call.	On his high horse.
To cut and run.	To take the bit in one's teeth.
Fits and starts.	At one fell swoop.
Over head and ears.	To take with a grain of salt.
At sixes and sevens.	In a nutshell.
By hook or by crook.	Be there with bells on.
To sink or swim.	A chip of the old block.
Off and on.	He is a bad egg.
As bold as brass.	All roads lead to Rome.
As cool as a cucumber.	To cudgel one's brains.
To cool one's heels.	To lend a hand.
Right off the reel.	As fit as a fiddle.
To show one's colors.	To take heart.
To keep your head.	To lose heart.
To keep your head above water.	To take to heart.
To lose your head.	To set your heart on.
To hold your head high.	To have at heart.
To hang your head.	To be the heart and soul of.
To have a head on your shoulders.	To have a soft (or hard) heart.
To have your head turned.	To give one's heart.
To have a swelled head.	To lose your heart.
To take into your head.	To win someone's heart.
To put out of your head.	To touch the heart of.
To put into someone's head.	To make one's heart leap.
To talk your head off.	To have a soft place in your heart.
To bite your head off.	To do your heart good.
To beat your head against a wall.	To have your heart in your mouth.
To throw yourself at the head of.	To wear your heart on your sleeve.
To put your head in a noose.	From the bottom of the heart.
To put your heads together.	With all one's heart.
To come to a head.	Sick at heart.
To bring—on your head.	Heavy of heart.
Head over heels.	Down hearted.
Head and shoulders above.	Heart-broken.
From head to foot.	Heart whole.

SENTENCES FOR PRACTICE.

Showing the English thought—and the Indian Sign equivalent.

ENGLISH. (In lower case) | INDIAN SIGN. (In capitals)

1. I like to swim. — I FOND SWIM.
2. You like to eat. — YOU FOND EAT.
3. We like to walk. — I ALL FOND WALK.
4. Fish swim under the water. — FISH SWIM BELOW WATER.
5. Beavers swim fast. — BEAVER SWIM FAST.
6. Scouts swim at camp. — SCOUT SWIM CAMP.
7. Horses eat grass. — HORSE EAT GRASS.
8. Dogs like to eat meat. — DOG FOND MEAT. EAT.
9. I eat with my father. — WITH MY FATHER, I EAT.
10. Two men are walking by the river. — TWO MAN WALK BESIDE RIVER.
11. Do you like to walk in the woods? — QUESTION YOU FOND WALK AMONG TREES?
12. Five boys are walking to camp. — FIVE BOY WALK CAMP.
13. The girl is running. — GIRL RUN.
14. The dog is running with the girl. — DOG RUN WITH GIRL.
15. Horses can run fast. — HORSE KNOW RUN FAST.
16. Do you know how to swim? — QUESTION YOU KNOW SWIM?
17. Can they build a fire? — QUESTION HE ALL KNOW MAKE FIRE?
18. I can read. — I UNDERSTAND READ.
19. Do you understand Indian Sign Language? — QUESTION YOU KNOW INDIAN SIGN LANGUAGE?
20. I understand a little. — I KNOW LITTLE.
21. Have you seen the horse? — QUESTION YOU SEE HORSE?
22. I have not seen the horse. — I HORSE SEE NOT.
23. Where are you going? — QUESTION WHERE YOU GO?
24. I am going to my home. — I GO MY HOUSE.
25. Your friend wants to go along. — YOUR FRIEND WANT GO WITH YOU.
26. Do you want to eat now? — QUESTION YOU WANT EAT NOW?
27. Not now, I am not hungry. — NOW NOT. I NO HUNGRY.
28. I want to get a drink of water. — I WANT WATER.
29. I want to go to sleep. — I WANT SLEEP.
30. Indians drink water from the river. — INDIAN GO RIVER. DRINK WATER.
31. They catch fish in the lake. — THEY TAKE FISH LAKE.
32. Look, it is raining. — SEE. RAIN.
33. Do you see the big dog? — QUESTION YOU SEE BIG DOG?
34. A cat sees well at night. — CAT SEE GOOD TOGETHER NIGHT.
35. I cannot see to work now. — I CANNOT SEE WORK NOW.
36. We like to work in summer. — I-ALL FOND WORK LONG-GRASS-TIME.
37. A girl must help her mother. — GIRL MUST WORK WITH MOTHER.
38. A good scout likes to help others. — GOOD SCOUT FOND WORK WITH ALL PEOPLE.
39. My sister does not want to cook supper. — MY SISTER WANT NOT MAKE EAT EVENING.
40. Can you make coffee? — QUESTION YOU KNOW MAKE COFFEE?
41. I will cut wood and build a fire. — I CHOP WOOD. MAKE FIRE.
42. When do we eat, at noon? — QUESTION FUTURE-TIME WE EAT, SUN HIGH?
43. I do not eat much for breakfast. — I EAT NOT MUCH SUNRISE.
44. All the smaller birds sleep at night. — ALL LITTLE BIRD SLEEP NIGHT.
45. The owl sleeps in the daytime and flies at night. — OWL SLEEP DAY. FLY NIGHT.
46. Bears sleep all winter. — BEAR MAKE BIG SLEEP COLD TIME.

47. How quietly the baby sleeps in its little bed.	BABY SLEEP QUIET LITTLE BED.
48. Last summer we went to the mountains.	LONG-GRASS-TIME BEYOND WE GO MOUNTAIN.
49. I like to see it snow in winter.	I FOND SEE SNOW WINTER.
50. We have lived here ten years.	TEN WINTER ME-ALL SIT TEEPEE HERE.
51. By brother is six years old.	MY BROTHER HAVE SIX WINTER.
52. The old Indian chief is very brave.	OLD INDIAN CHIEF MUCH BRAVE.
53. The old flag waves over the church.	OLD FLAG FLY ABOVE GOD-HOUSE.
54. Come here and look at the moon.	COME HERE, SEE MOON.
55. We see the moon and the stars at night.	ME-ALL SEE MOON WITH MANY STAR NIGHT.
56. Only the sun shines today.	ALONE SUN WORK GOOD DAY NOW.
57. I would rather walk alone.	I WANT WALK ALONE.
58. I have only one brother.	I HAVE ONE ALONE BROTHER.
59. My only brother is very strong.	MY ALONE BROTHER MUCH STRONG.
60. The soldier has only one son.	SOLDIER HAVE ONE ALONE SON.
61. Little girls often laugh.	LITTLE GIRL LAUGH OFTEN.
62. We often see the soldiers march.	WE SEE SOLDIER WALK OFTEN.
63. Birds sing frequently in the Spring.	BIRD SING OFTEN SHORT-GRASS-TIME.
64. Are you an Arapahoe?	QUESTION YOU ARAPAHOE?
65. No, I am a Cheyenne chief.	NO I CHEYENNE CHIEF.
66. What is your name?	QUESTION YOU CALLED?
67. My name is Big Beaver.	I CALLED BIG BEAVER.
68. I would like to know your name.	I FOND KNOW YOU CALLED.
69. My name is White Crow.	I CALLED WHITE CROW.
70. I am an Arapahoe scout.	I SCOUT. ARAPAHOE.
71. Where do you live?	QUESTION WHERE YOU SIT?
72. I live across the mountains.	I SIT ACROSS MOUNTAIN.
73. What are you doing here?	QUESTION YOU WORK HERE?
74. I am hunting beaver.	I HUNT BEAVER.
75. Have you caught any?	QUESTION YOU TAKE BEAVER?
76. No, the beavers are all gone.	NO. BEAVER ALL GONE.
77. Did you see any white men to-day?	QUESTION YOU SEE WHITE MAN DAY NOW?
78. Yes, on the other side of the mountain.	YES. ACROSS MOUNTAIN.
79. How many did you see?	QUESTION MANY YOU SEE?
80. I saw one, alone.	I SEE ONE. ALONE.
81. Was he a young man?	QUESTION WHITE MAN FEW WINTER?
82. No, he was very old.	NO. WHITE MAN MUCH OLD.
83. What was he doing?	QUESTION WHITE MAN DO?
84. He was leading two horses.	WHITE MAN LEAD TWO HORSE.
85. Where did he go?	QUESTION WHERE HE GO?
86. He went up the river.	WHITE MAN GO UP RIVER.
87. We are holding a council tonight.	WE SIT COUNCIL NIGHT NOW.
88. Good, can I sit in?	GOOD. QUESTION I SIT WITH YOU?
89. Yes, all chiefs are welcome.	YES. WE FOND ALL CHIEF SIT WITH US.
90. Where does your council meet?	QUESTION WHERE YOU SIT COUNCIL?
91. Among the trees.	AMONG TREES.
92. Where are the trees?	QUESTION WHERE TREES?
93. Over the river, beside the mountain.	ACROSS RIVER, BESIDE MOUNTAIN.
94. Are you hungry?	QUESTION YOU HUNGRY?
95. Yes, I had no breakfast.	YES. I NO EAT SUNRISE.

96. I have plenty of food.	I HAVE PLENTY FOOD.
97. Good, where is it?	GOOD. QUESTION WHERE?
98. At my teepee.	MY TEEPEE.
99. All right, let's go.	GOOD, WE GO.
100. You are my good friend.	YOU GOOD FRIEND.
101. Before the white man came, many buffalo roamed the plains.	TIME-PAST MANY BUFFALO WALK ACROSS PRAIRIE; TIME-FUTURE WHITEMAN COME.
102. After the white man came, the buffalo disappeared.	TIME-PAST WHITEMAN COME, TIME-FUTURE BUFFALO ALL GONE.
103. Now cattle feed where once the buffalo roamed.	NOW SPOTTED BUFFALO EAT WHERE TIME-PAST BUFFALO WALK.
104. Don't wait for me, I'll come pretty soon.	WAIT ME NOT. I COME SHORT-TIME FUTURE.
105. I will sit here and read until he finishes his work.	I SIT, READ. FUTURE-TIME HE FINISH WORK.
106. I should like to see a beaver when it starts to cut down a tree.	I WANT SEE BEAVER TIME-FUTURE BEGIN CUT TREE.
107. May the Great Spirit permit your moccasins to make tracks in many snows.	GREAT MYSTERY HELP YOUR MOCCASIN MAKE TRACK ABOARD SNOW LONG-TIME.
108. May the Great Scoutmaster of all good scouts be with us all now and forever.	GREAT MYSTERY ALL GOOD SCOUT SIT WITH YOU—ALL NOW AND FOREVER.
109. When do we go on our overnight hike to scout camp?	QUESTION FUTURE-TIME WE WALK SCOUT CAMP? STAY. SLEEP CAMP.
110. The Pawnees had a chief whose name was Spotted Bull.	TIME-PAST PAWNEE HAVE CHIEF CALLED SPOTTED-MALE-BUFFALO.
11. Spotted Bull aroused the Pawnees to make war on the Sioux.	SPOTTED-MALE-BUFFALO MAKE BIG TALK. SAY PAWNEE MUST MAKE WAR SIOUX.
112. The Pawnees had many good warriors, also horses and rifles.	PAWNEE HAVE MANY BRAVE WARRIOR WITH MANY HORSE MANY GUN.
113. The Pawnees built up their own courage by vilifying the Sioux.	PAWNEE MAKE OWN HEART STRONG. ABUSE SIOUX.
114. The Pawnees said that the Sioux men were squaws and didn't know how to fight, and that the Sioux made weak medicine.	PAWNEE SAY SIOUX MAN EQUAL WOMAN, UNDERSTAND FIGHT NO. MAKE STRONG MEDICINE NO.
115. Spotted Bull, the Pawnee Chief, stole many horses and took them across the little Snake River.	SPOTTED MALE BUFFALO. CHIEF PAWNEE, STEAL MANY HORSE. MAKE HORSE GO ACROSS LITTLE SNAKE RIVER.
116. The Sioux saw the trail, followed it for many days and put up a big fight.	SIOUX SEE TRAIL, FOLLOW TRAIL MANY SLEEP, MAKE BIG FIGHT.
117. They killed nine Pawnees, took all the Sioux and Pawnee horses, and went back to the Sioux camp.	THEY KILL NINE PAWNEE, TAKE ALL SIOUX HORSE, ALL PAWNEE HORSE, GO CAMP SIOUX.
118. The Pawnees were ready to quit.	PAWNEE WANT STOP FIGHT.
119. They called a council with the Sioux and made peace.	THEY SIT COUNCIL WITH SIOUX. ALL MAKE PEACE.
120. It looks like rain today, we'll start our deer hunt tomorrow.	PERHAPS RAIN DAY NOW, WE GO TOMORROW HUNT DEER.
121. If the snow is deep the birds cannot find food to eat.	PERHAPS SNOW MUCH, BIRD CANNOT SEE TAKE EAT.
122. If you want to go with us, you must be ready at noon.	PERHAPS YOU WANT GO WITH US, YOU MUST GO NOON.
123. Did you speak to me? Yes, I told you to follow me.	QUESTION YOU SPEAK ME? YES I SAY YOU FOLLOW ME.

124. Wait a moment. You cannot speak while everyone is chattering.

WAIT LITTLE. YOU CANNOT SPEAK, ALL PEOPLE LITTLE TALK.

125. Be quiet, listen to the speaker.

QUIET: LISTEN: MAN TALK.

126. Tell your secrets only to your friends.

ALONE WITH FRIEND TALK SECRET.

127. Very many Sioux Indians are good singers and dancers.

MANY SIOUX SING DANCE GOOD.

128. The bird builds its nest in a tree.

BIRD MAKE HOUSE ABOARD TREE.

129. The black bear grows very big.

BEAR COLOR BLACK GROW MUCH BIG.

130. For many days the forest fire burned fiercely.

FOREST FIRE BURN STRONG LONG-TIME.

131. The man is poor and blind.

MAN HAVE MONEY NOT, SEE NOT, EYE WIPED OUT.

132. A bad man stole my fine horse to-day.

MAN, HEART BAD, STEAL MY GOOD HORSE DAY NOW.

133. The Indian ran all the way home, and when he reached home was very tired.

INDIAN RUN HOUSE, ARRIVE-THERE MUCH TIRED.

134. White men labor hard to make money.

WHITE MAN WORK MUCH, EFFORT GET MONEY.

135. When the wind blows hard, the fire burns brightly.

WIND GO FAST. FIRE BURN STRONG.

136. What did the dog eat last evening?

QUESTION DOG EAT YESTERDAY SUN-SET?

137. The old woman went to the farmer to get some corn.

WOMAN OLD GO FARM-MAN, BRING CORN.

138. Today I saw a large flock of blackbirds roosting in a tree.

DAY NOW I SEE MANY LITTLE BIRD COLOR BLACK SIT TREE.

139. Children love to sing and dance and laugh.

LITTLE BOY LITTLE GIRL FOND SING DANCE LAUGH.

140. The Dakota Chief, Crazy Horse, was a fearless man and lived in the Sioux country on Cheyenne River.

DAKOTA CHIEF CALLED CRAZY HORSE SIT SIOUX COUNTRY BE-SIDE GOOD RIVER.

For a long time I have been wanting to get a place for a mountain camp. Last summer I found a place that I thought would do very well. It was all wooded; it had a creek running through it; and there was a beautiful spot for a camp. The owner wanted $500.00, and I bought it on the spot.

LONG-TIME-PAST I WANT BUY LITTLE LAND MOUNTAIN MAKE CAMP. LONG-GRASS-TIME BEYOND I SEE LITTLE LAND I THINK GOOD. LIT-TLE-LAND POSSESS MANY TREES, POSSESS RIVER-LITTLE, MAKE BEAUTIFUL CAMP. MAN WANT SELL LITTLE-LAND FIVE HUND-RED MONEY. I BUY LITTLE-LAND.

Two months ago I took two friends with me and went up to start the camp. The day we got there we saw tracks of deer and bear, and caught some fish for supper. We were too tired when night came to put up our tents, and we didn't think it would rain anyway. We made up our beds near the fire and lay down to sleep.

TWO MOON BEYOND I WITH TWO FRIEND GO MAKE-RISE CAMP. WE ARRIVE LITTLE-LAND; WE SEE TRACK DEER, BEAR; WE TAKE FISH EAT SUNSET. EVENING COME WE TIRED. WE WANT NOT MAKE RISE TENT; WE THINK RAIN NO. WE MAKE BED NEAR FIRE, SLEEP.

In the middle of the night it began to rain. Before daylight we were soaking wet. One of my friends got sick, and there was no doctor anywhere near. Much to our disgust, we had to break camp and come back home.

MIDDLE NIGHT BEGIN RAIN. MORN-ING COME, WE ALL MUCH WATER. ONE FRIEND ARRIVE AT SICK. WHITE - CHIEF - MEDICINE NEAR NO. HEART MUCH TIRED, WE MUST STOP SIT CAMP, COME HOME.

VITALIZING A SIGN LANGUAGE PROGRAM TO FIT
A BOY SCOUT TROOP MEETING PROGRAM

Boys are always interested in mystery, secrecy, and all things that are beyond the comprehension. Sign language can be made a vital part of the troop,—for building troop spirit and troop interest.

1. Instead of allowing scouts to enter the troop room helter-skelter, have the Senior Patrol Leader, or one of the troop officers, receive the scout at the door and ask him, in sign language, "Who are you?" To which he responds in sign language, "I am a good scout." Answering, the Leader says, "Good, come in." This continues until all the boys are received. Then there may be two or three new lads who do not know the sign, and of course will have a profound desire to learn it. The Scoutmaster then has the opportunity, which is most important, of meeting these new lads and bringing them into the troop. It is quite common for boys to deny other boys getting in on the inside. The Scoutmaster then steps across, gives these boys a short talk, tells them some of the intricacies of the scout program, and how they can become regular fellows and get into the troop.

2. Let us now consider the scout that comes in late, interrupts the meeting, attracts attention. He may break the trend of thought under consideration, especially if he goes up and talks with the Scoutmaster and explains why he is tardy, etc. Instead, let him come in in regular form, approach the flag, salute it, salute the Scoutmaster, and in sign language say he is sorry, (heart on the ground), that he wants to come in.

3. Build into each patrol, patrol sign language which all the members of the patrol will understand. This will help toward building patrol spirit, and a unity within the troop having its origin within the patrol.

4. Ceremonial, also initiation. For these we have regular suggested forms.

5. As an alternative, when there is possibly only one to introduce, the tenderfoot can be brought into the room by a scout who offers him as a member. The scout who brings the candidate in may say: "I bring this boy, make good scout." This will be mysterious to the candidate, will keep him guessing as to what is being said about him, will show him that there is something to learn and understand, and will inspire him to come through a hundred per cent in order to measure up to the mysticism that surrounds the ceremonial. After two or three questions have been exchanged and answered, the candidate is then received into the program and is relieved of any anxiety and told that he may now become a regular member, etc. He should then be turned over to whoever is in charge of the sign language work, and be properly prepared and taught some of the mysteries of the troop program. This should not be confused in any way with secrecy or with the secret fraternity idea.

6. Instead of the usual method of scouts attention, or scouts alert, form a straight line. The leader puts forth his hands, giving the signal for calling attention. He then gives the order:

> A. Stand.
> B. Sit down.
> C. Attention.
> D. Look at Bulletin Board.
> E. Return to Patrol Formation.

7. Signs or signals can be given for troop on the move. Signal to call patrol leaders to Big Chief. Signal for calling patrols in circle formation. Signal for calling "Troop circle formation." Signal for "Straight line formation." Signal for "Sit down for an Indian story." Signal for "Council meeting of troop officers and patrol leaders."

The foregoing ideas are possible of an immense variety of treatment, and can as well be adapted to the use of Girl Scouts, Campfire Girls, Rangers, or any organization of youth.

SUGGESTED TROOP PROGRAM

Before 7:30—DUMB BELL TAG. The players stand scattered about the playing area one of their number being "it" and is placed in the center of the area. A dumb bell or some similar object is passed from one player to another, "it" attempting to tag the player who has the dumb bell. If he succeeds, the one being tagged is "it".

7:30—Fall in. Roll call. Collection of dues. Inspection. Flag ceremony.

7:40—SAFETY DRILLS. Make your troop patrols rescue crews. Dramatize ice or water rescues, electric accidents, automobile accidents, etc. Explain mistakes afterwards—make an inter-patrol contest out of it.

8:00—PATROL MEETING. Have some of your best sign talkers teach each of your patrols the Indian Sign Language.
Instruct scouts in test passing for the court of honor.

8:20—Develop Indian Sign Language through games or stunts, and prepare them for passing the Signaling tests for second or first class; also for the sign language part and the Indian games portion of the new Indian Lore Merit Badge. Give the playlet to some of your best sign talkers and let them put it on.

8:50—Announcements. Scoutmasters 5 minutes. Read or talk on citizenship. Scout handbook pages 532-540.

9:00—Fall in. Hand salute. Indian Sign Language Benediction. Troop dismissed.

INDIAN CEREMONY FOR OPENING COUNCIL FIRE

TWO BOY SCOUTS, FOUR INDIANS. THEY ENTER FROM DIFFERENT POINTS

Each Boy Scout holds up his hand and says: "How."
Each Indian holds up his right hand and says: "How."
INDIAN CHIEF: "What wants the paleface in the land of the Indian?"
BOY SCOUT: "We desire to camp here, oh chief, to live in the open as your people have done, and to hold our council fire among these hills during the Red Moon and the Falling Leaf Moon, even as the Indians did here a long time ago."
CHIEF: "Friends, this is the hunting ground of my forefathers. Many moons, long ago, they roamed these hills, pitched their teepees in these valleys,and the smoke of their council fires drifted above these tree tops.
"In great numbers they trod this trail to the lodge of their chief, from here but a short journey. Upon this very hill lies the tomb of our Chief.
"My people were the friends of the animals, of the birds, the flowers and the trees. They clothed us, sustained us and protected us. We respected all living creatures. We left the woods and the fields as we found them. We ask that the White Man use these council grounds the way the Indian did. If he do so, we are glad the White Man is here. I have spoken."
BOY SCOUT: "We promise, oh chief, to protect everything that grows and lives in the woods and fields of your ancestors. We will try to leave it as we found it, so that it may be enjoyed by those who come after us. I have said it."
Sometime before the meeting have drawn on the ground, within the circle, with whiting or lime, an outline of a snake. Then, at this point, the Chief rubs out the snake with his foot and says: "We now destroy the snake with all it represents—with its forked tongue— as there is no room for untruth or hatred here."
Chief gives the signs for: "I give you the Sun. I give you the Moon. I give you the Deer, the Elk, the Bear, the Wolf, the Birds; I give you the council fire. I am your friend."

FIRE LIGHTING

Indians seated on the ground at side, each with a leafy branch. Each one in turn dances around the fire, using the toe-heel and other two-step counts, then lays his branch on top of the fire and returns to place.

Fire lighter prepares fire lighting set, while a Boy Scout or an Indian tells some kind of an appropriate story, such as, "How the Coyote Stole the Fire." Or the fire can slide down a wire from a place where it is concealed in a tree.

As soon as the story is finished, the fire should be lit.

Those who participated in the act then say, "How" and exit.

(The entire proceedings should be in charge of a Chief who wears a headdress and any other Indian equipment possible.)

SOME SIGN LANGUAGE SUGGESTIONS

In the West, where the writer has taught in many places, they make much use of sign language. When two boys or girls leave camp or town on a hike they, in many cases, go pledged from their departure until their return to communicate in no way except in sign language. At camp fires and troop meetings they evolve little plays, games and contests in sign language, thereby developing its practicability and its charm. All of this adds mystery and spirit, and helps to strengthen a program.

HERE IS A SUGGESTION FOR A POSSIBLE PLAY IN THE INDIAN SIGN LANGUAGE

By William Tomkins

The scene is somewhere in the wilderness. A father and son have been camping together. Going out on a hunt they get lost and cannot find camp. They meet an Indian. (You can costume the Indian with a blanket and one or two feathers in a head band.) The play opens as father and son walk out on the stage.

Father: "Well, son, it looks as if we are lost in the wilderness."

Son: "Yes, dad, we have been lost for three days now."

Father: "Unless something happens we are sure to perish."

Son: "Yes. I'm hungry and am afraid we'll starve."

The Indian walks in.

Father: "Hello, Mr. Indian, I'm glad you came. We are lost. How can we get out of here?"

Indian: "No sabe." (This is said with fingers to his lips.)

Father: "Isn't there anyone around here that speaks English?"

Indian: "No sabe."

Son: "Say, dad, maybe he knows Indian sign."

Father: "Do you know it?"

Son: "Yes, I learned it in Scouting."

Father: "Well, go ahead; try it."

Son: (Indian sign) "Do you understand Indian sign language?"

Indian: (Indian sign) "Yes, I understand."

Son: "It's all right, dad; he says he knows it. What shall I ask him now?"

Father: "Why, tell him we're lost."

Son: (I. S.) "We're lost."

Indian: (I. S.) "No, you no lost, you here."

Son: "Dad, he says we're not lost; we're here."

Father: "Well, I guess he's right at that. Tell him we went out hunting and can't find our camp."

Son: (I. S.) "We go hunt. Cannot find camp."

Indian: (I. S.) "Where is your camp?"

Son: "Dad, he wants to know where our camp is."

Father: "That's just what I don't know. Tell him it's by a lake."

Son: (I. S.) "We make-rise tent beside lake."

Indian: (I. S.) "Me understand. Three lakes beside here."

Son: "He says there are three lakes near here."

Father: "Tell him it's a little lake near a big mountain."

Son: (I. S.) "Little lake beside big mountain."

Indian: (I. S.) "I understand. Go not now; night come fast. Stay (sit) with me. Future time one sleep I go with you."

Son: "He says he knows where it is, Dad, but it's too late to go now. He says to stay with him and he'll go with us tomorrow."

Father: "All right; we stay. I'm tired and hungry anyway."

Son: (I. S.) "Good, we stay with you."

Indian: (I. S.) "Perhaps you hungry. Come with me. I give you food."

Son: "He says if we're hungry, Dad, to go with him and he'll give us food."

Father: "All right, let's go."

All Exit.

SUGGESTION FOR INDIAN SIGN LANGUAGE PLAYLET

A company of soldiers is camped on the prairie in the Indian country. An Indian Scout, exhausted, reaches camp and tells of some recent trouble between two hostile bands of Sioux and Cheyenne. After he has rested and recovered somewhat, he tells the story in sign.

THE STORY	INDIAN SIGN EQUIVALENT
Indian Scout: "I was traveling over the prairie when down in the Cheyenne River valley I saw two bands of Indians meet. I know they are Sioux and Cheyenne, because they come from Sioux and Cheyenne camps. Two chiefs ride out and meet and converse for a long time, but evidently did not agree. They rode back to their friends and soon they all start shooting. I think it perhaps because Sioux stole many Cheyenne horses."	*INDIAN SCOUT:* "I RIDE OVER PRAIRIE. GO GOOD RIVER VALLEY. SEE MANY INDIANS WANT FIGHT. MANY SIOUX. MANY CHEYENNE. COME SIOUX CHEYENNE CAMP. TWO CHIEF RIDE. MEET. TALK LONG TIME. GO WITH FRIENDS. START SHOOT. I THINK PERHAPS SIOUX STOLE MANY CHEYENNE HORSE."
Captain: "Where are the Indians now?"	*CAPTAIN:* "QUESTION WHERE INDIANS NOW?"
Scout: "Across prairie, beside Cheyenne River."	*SCOUT:* "ACROSS PRAIRIE BESIDE GOOD RIVER."
Captain: "Where is your horse?"	*CAPTAIN:* "QUESTION WHERE YOUR HORSE?"
Scout: "Horse swim river, climb mountain. go across prairie; horse foot go down prairie dog hole, break foot; shoot horse. I feel very bad."	*SCOUT:* "HORSE SWIM RIVER. CLIMB MOUNTAIN. GO ACROSS PRAIRIE. HORSE FOOT GO DOWN PRAIRIE DOG HOLE. BREAK FOOT. SHOOT HORSE. ME HEART ON THE GROUND."
Captain: "What do you think the Indians will do now?"	*CAPTAIN:* "WHAT YOU THINK INDIANS DO NOW?"
Scout: "I think perhaps the Indians will go to the Fort and attack the soldiers."	*SCOUT:* "PERHAPS INDIANS GO FORT. MAKE FIGHT WITH SOLDIERS."
They all start for the Fort. On the way they meet the two bands of Indians, who are coming along together.	ALL START FOR FORT. THEY MEET THE TWO BANDS OF INDIANS COMING ALONG TOGETHER.
Captain, to Indians: "I thought you people were fighting?"	*CAPTAIN:* "I UNDERSTAND YOU INDIANS ALL FIGHT?"
Sioux Chief: "We fight a little while and then understand it is bad medicine; so we hold a council and make peace."	*SIOUX CHIEF:* "YES. INDIANS FIGHT LITTLE WHILE. ALL UNDERSTAND FIGHT BAD MEDICINE. HOLD COUNCIL. MAKE PEACE."
Cheyenne Chief: "Sioux Chief speaks the truth; his tongue is not crooked like a snake. All Cheyenne and Sioux Indians make peace and now live like friends."	*CHEYENNE CHIEF:* "SIOUX CHIEF TALK TRUE. TONGUE NO CROOKED LIKE SNAKE. ALL CHEYENNE SIOUX MAKE PEACE. NOW FRIENDS, BROTHERS."

INDIAN CEREMONIAL INITIATION FOR BOY SCOUTS

By William Tomkins

PROPERTIES.

Blanket or other drapery for each Scout. It is desirable that Tenderfoot Scouts wear one feather, Second Class Scouts—two, and First Class Scouts—three. Scoutmasters and assistants should have more pretentious display, if possible (this can be an old shirt, fringed and decorated with paint, etc., or made-up costumes, war bonnet). If possible have an electric or other council fire. Have a Tom-Tom, or a portable phonograph with Indian music.

STAGE SETTING.

Troop in Indian regalia seated in circle around fire, at distance of 15 feet. Chief and assistants at fire within circle, according to diagram.

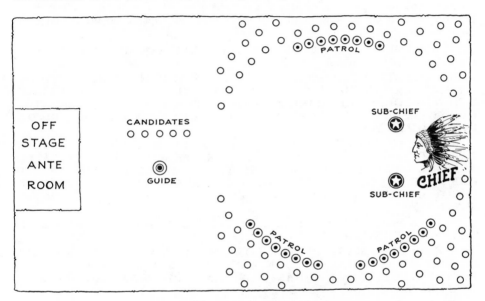

Lights out, or very dim. Fire in operation.

ACTION.

One of the assistants, or any combination of assistants or boys do an Indian dance, to Tom-Tom or primitive music on portable phonograph, or have the music alone. All this is optional and according to individual possibilities, but highly recommended.

All conversation around the fire is in sign language and therefore silent. A reader in the back of the audience will interpret the gestures.

Guide enters with candidates. Halts them and comes close to outside of circle. Makes sign of friendly greeting.

Chief invites him to come within circle, using sign language.

Guide signs that he has come a long ways, over mountains (meaning the tests), across a river (meaning the parents' consent), with boys who want to make themselves Scouts (or with boys who want to sit at the council fire).

Chief signs for boys to be brought to the fire.

This is done by motion, by the guide.

Chief (in sign): "Why want go with scouts?"

Candidates (Being scouts they are supposed to know the sign language): "Want go woods, make me strong, brave, true; rise in the world." (Be a rising man.)

The Chief and his assistants rise to their feet.

Chief: "Make scout oath."

Candidates make the oath in sign language,—all may do it at once, or the candidates may do it while the rest hold the oath sign.

Chief makes sign: "Good."

Chief pins tenderfoot pin on each candidate, then makes sign: "YOU, ME, ALL

BROTHERS, NOW, ALWAYS." Chief makes sign of shaking hands. He then motions to scouts in each patrol, some members of which will come forward, (as many as there are candidates), throw one arm and blanket over a candidate's shoulder, and bring him to a place in the circle.

Then everybody will rise and give the Scout benediction in sign, or do a friendship dance, followed by the benediction.

SIGN LANGUAGE EXERCISES SUITABLE FOR PASSING TESTS

There are a number of sentences which can be made up of the signs included in the first 150 signs taught by William Tomkins in his lessons. These are also found among the signs on page 64 of the Tomkins book. By learning the 200 signs on page 64 one can become quite fluent in the use of sign language. The following stories or sentences will enable anyone to pass the first class test; in fact there are four times as many as necessary for this, or to do the sign language required for the Indian Lore Merit Badge.

I SEE YOU ALL COME HERE TODAY. NOW SEE ME TALK INDIAN SIGN LANGUAGE. HAVE GOOD TIME.

WHERE YOU GO? I GO HOME. WHY? I WANT EAT. I WANT DRINK. I WANT SLEEP. I WANT GO MAKE CAMP. WHAT YOU DO—CAMPING? I CHOP WOOD. I MAKE FIRE. I MAKE COFFEE. I GO WALK. I GO RUN. I GO SWIM. I GO HUNT. I SEE DEER, ELK, BEAR, BEAVER, WOLF, BIRDS. I HAVE GOOD TIME.

I RIDE HORSE ACROSS MOUNTAIN. GO ACROSS RIVER. GO ACROSS LAKE. GO AMONG TREES. SEE FIVE DEER. SEE FOUR ELK. SEE THREE BEAR. SEE TWO BEAVER. SEE ONE WOLF. SEE FIVE BIRDS. SHOOT ONE DEER. SHOOT ONE ELK. SHOOT ONE BEAR. SHOOT ONE BEAVER. SHOOT ONE WOLF. SHOOT FIVE BIRDS. COME HOME, EAT, DRINK, SLEEP.

TODAY NOW I TRADE HORSE WITH INDIAN CHIEF. INDIAN CHIEF TRADE HORSE WITH ME.

TODAY NOW MANY PEOPLE COME HERE HAVE GOOD TIME. SEE BOY SCOUT TALK INDIAN SIGN LANGUAGE. BOY SCOUT WANT ALL PEOPLE UNDERSTAND INDIAN SIGN LANGUAGE. WANT ALL PEOPLE TALK SIGN LANGUAGE GOOD.

LONG TIME AGO INDIAN BAD. LONG TIME AGO WHITE MAN BAD. MAKE BIG FIGHT LONG TIME. NOW INDIAN GOOD. NOW WHITE MAN GOOD. MAYBE SO. MAKE PEACE. FIGHT NOT.

I SEE ALL YOU GOOD PEOPLE. GOOD FATHER. GOOD MOTHER. GOOD FRIEND. ALL COME HERE SEE SCOUTS. MAKE MEDICINE. SEE ALL SCOUTS WORK GOOD. MAKE FIRE. MAKE FOOD. TALK INDIAN SIGN LANGUAGE. HAVE SUNRISE IN HEART.

THREE CHEYENNE INDIAN BOY GO HUNT. COME SIOUX COUNTRY. SIOUX MAKE WAR. THREE BOY SCOUT WALK QUIET. TALK SIGN LANGUAGE. SIOUX SCOUT SEE BOY. GO TELL SIOUX CHIEF. CHIEF TELL MEN GO TAKE THREE BOY. BOY SEE MEN COME. RUN FAST ABOARD HILL. THREE BOY MAKE MANY BIG ROCK ROLL DOWN HILL. KILL FIVE SIOUX. THREE BOY GO CHEYENNE COUNTRY FAST. SLEEP TWO NIGHT. SEE MOUNTAIN GOAT. KILL ONE GOAT. EAT. GO HOME. MANY CHEYENNE HEART SUNRISE.

GREAT SCOUT MASTER, ALL GOOD SCOUTS BE WITH YOU ALL NOW, FOREVER.

(To sing Taps.) DAY DONE. GONE SUN. GO LAKE. GO HILL. GO TREE. ALL GOOD. PEACE SLEEP. GREAT MYSTERY HERE.

IMMORTALITY

By WILLIAM TOMKINS

[So many Scout Executives, Service Club Members and others have asked for a copy of the following poem that the author gives it herewith.]

Some think this world a vale of tears, or worry and of sighs;
    That Life's a great big lottery, in which few win a prize.
I read some hopeless verses once that don't deserve to last,—
    They told how the mill can never grind with water that is past.

I'd like to change that fallacy which has caused so many a tear,
    And by transposing make it bear a message of good cheer
And point the way of winds of hope, like pennant on a mast,
    For I know that the mill can grind again with water that is past.

A mountain stream comes trickling in the sunlight down the hill,
    And gathers volume until it has strength to run the mill;
It happily continues then, upon its useful way,—
    Turns other mills still further down, until it joins the bay.

Its temporary mission o'er, it sweeps out to the sea
    With other useful waters bearing it company;
And there all peacefully they rest, beneath the shining sun.
    Who seems to think their mission is scarcely yet begun.

With gentle force He lifts them up in vapors to the sky,
    And gathers them in fleecy clouds in His domain so high,
Where kindly winds then waft them back to that mountain home,
    From which a few short hours before we saw them start to roam.

The cooling night then causes them to fall in gentle showers,
    A blessing to that mountainside, to grass and trees and flowers;
And in the dawn of early morn we find them back once more
    In that same little mountainside, but stronger than before.

They gather volume as they come a-tumbling down the hill,
    And then with added vigor again they turn the mill;
And then in play they rush away, through meadowland and town,
    And every mill again is turned as they go dancing down.

The brightest day is no more useful than the darkest night,—
    Our troubles soon would disappear if we'd view them aright.
Good fortune may be holding back her best things to the last,
    For I know that the mill can grind again with water that is past.

    And that same little mountain stream
        Has always been to me
    But one of Nature's many proofs
        Of Immortality.

A Word to Advanced Students

A good sign talker can carry on a conversation in sign about three times as fast as he could speak and at least six times faster than any wigwag or semaphore system now in use could transmit the same message.

To merely know a given number of signs, however, is still a long way from being a good sign talker or being able to use the various combinations with proper accent and understanding.

Sign language deals with ideas rather than words and the literal meaning of each unit or individual sign depends upon what signs it is used with. The sign for QUESTION, for instance, may mean WHY, WHERE, WHEN, WHAT, WHO or HOW MANY, CAN YOU, WILL YOU, according to the sense in which it is used. The sign for EAT may mean either TO EAT or FOOD, and the gesture for POSSESSION covers all words denoting possession or ownership.

Each sign should be considered as a GENERAL IDEA UNIT which acquires a literal and definite meaning only when associated with certain other signs. In other words, each sign is a kind of idea alphabet block, to be placed end to end with other blocks when by their association a definite meaning is established.

In the same way, a compound sign might be illustrated by placing its block elements side by side as one unit in the main line of thought.

It will be seen from the foregoing wherein signs differ from words. For in a list of synonyms each word has a definite meaning inherent in itself, while a single sign may mean any one of its synonyms, according to the other signs with which it is placed, and which determine its precise meaning.

A CATALOG OF SELECTED
DOVER BOOKS
IN ALL FIELDS OF INTEREST

A CATALOG OF SELECTED DOVER
BOOKS IN ALL FIELDS OF INTEREST

DRAWINGS OF REMBRANDT, edited by Seymour Slive. Updated Lippmann, Hofstede de Groot edition, with definitive scholarly apparatus. All portraits, biblical sketches, landscapes, nudes. Oriental figures, classical studies, together with selection of work by followers. 550 illustrations. Total of 630pp. 9⅛ × 12¼.
21485-0, 21486-9 Pa., Two-vol. set $25.00

GHOST AND HORROR STORIES OF AMBROSE BIERCE, Ambrose Bierce. 24 tales vividly imagined, strangely prophetic, and decades ahead of their time in technical skill: "The Damned Thing," "An Inhabitant of Carcosa," "The Eyes of the Panther," "Moxon's Master," and 20 more. 199pp. 5⅜ × 8½. 20767-6 Pa. $3.95

ETHICAL WRITINGS OF MAIMONIDES, Maimonides. Most significant ethical works of great medieval sage, newly translated for utmost precision, readability. Laws Concerning Character Traits, Eight Chapters, more. 192pp. 5⅜ × 8½.
24522-5 Pa. $4.50

THE EXPLORATION OF THE COLORADO RIVER AND ITS CANYONS, J. W. Powell. Full text of Powell's 1,000-mile expedition down the fabled Colorado in 1869. Superb account of terrain, geology, vegetation, Indians, famine, mutiny, treacherous rapids, mighty canyons, during exploration of last unknown part of continental U.S. 400pp. 5⅜ × 8½. 20094-9 Pa. $6.95

HISTORY OF PHILOSOPHY, Julián Marías. Clearest one-volume history on the market. Every major philosopher and dozens of others, to Existentialism and later. 505pp. 5⅜ × 8½. 21739-6 Pa. $8.50

ALL ABOUT LIGHTNING, Martin A. Uman. Highly readable non-technical survey of nature and causes of lightning, thunderstorms, ball lightning, St. Elmo's Fire, much more. Illustrated. 192pp. 5⅜ × 8½. 25237-X Pa. $5.95

SAILING ALONE AROUND THE WORLD, Captain Joshua Slocum. First man to sail around the world, alone, in small boat. One of great feats of seamanship told in delightful manner. 67 illustrations. 294pp. 5⅜ × 8½. 20326-3 Pa. $4.95

LETTERS AND NOTES ON THE MANNERS, CUSTOMS AND CONDI-TIONS OF THE NORTH AMERICAN INDIANS, George Catlin. Classic account of life among Plains Indians: ceremonies, hunt, warfare, etc. 312 plates. 572pp. of text. 6⅛ × 9¼. 22118-0, 22119-9 Pa. Two-vol. set $15.90

ALASKA: The Harriman Expedition, 1899, John Burroughs, John Muir, et al. Informative, engrossing accounts of two-month, 9,000-mile expedition. Native peoples, wildlife, forests, geography, salmon industry, glaciers, more. Profusely illustrated. 240 black-and-white line drawings. 124 black-and-white photographs. 3 maps. Index. 576pp. 5⅜ × 8½. 25109-8 Pa. $11.95

SUNDIALS, Albert Waugh. Far and away the best, most thorough coverage of ideas, mathematics concerned, types, construction, adjusting anywhere. Over 100 illustrations. 230pp. 5⅜ × 8½. 22947-5 Pa. $4.50

PICTURE HISTORY OF THE NORMANDIE: With 190 Illustrations, Frank O. Braynard. Full story of legendary French ocean liner: Art Deco interiors, design innovations, furnishings, celebrities, maiden voyage, tragic fire, much more. Extensive text. 144pp. 8⅜ × 11¾. 25257-4 Pa. $9.95

THE FIRST AMERICAN COOKBOOK: A Facsimile of "American Cookery," 1796, Amelia Simmons. Facsimile of the first American-written cookbook published in the United States contains authentic recipes for colonial favorites—pumpkin pudding, winter squash pudding, spruce beer, Indian slapjacks, and more. Introductory Essay and Glossary of colonial cooking terms. 80pp. 5⅜ × 8½. 24710-4 Pa. $3.50

101 PUZZLES IN THOUGHT AND LOGIC, C. R. Wylie, Jr. Solve murders and robberies, find out which fishermen are liars, how a blind man could possibly identify a color—purely by your own reasoning! 107pp. 5⅜ × 8½. 20367-0 Pa. $2.50

THE BOOK OF WORLD-FAMOUS MUSIC—CLASSICAL, POPULAR AND FOLK, James J. Fuld. Revised and enlarged republication of landmark work in musico-bibliography. Full information about nearly 1,000 songs and compositions including first lines of music and lyrics. New supplement. Index. 800pp. 5⅜ × 8¼. 24857-7 Pa. $14.95

ANTHROPOLOGY AND MODERN LIFE, Franz Boas. Great anthropologist's classic treatise on race and culture. Introduction by Ruth Bunzel. Only inexpensive paperback edition. 255pp. 5⅜ × 8½. 25245-0 Pa. $5.95

THE TALE OF PETER RABBIT, Beatrix Potter. The inimitable Peter's terrifying adventure in Mr. McGregor's garden, with all 27 wonderful, full-color Potter illustrations. 55pp. 4¼ × 5½. (Available in U.S. only) 22827-4 Pa. $1.75

THREE PROPHETIC SCIENCE FICTION NOVELS, H. G. Wells. *When the Sleeper Wakes, A Story of the Days to Come* and *The Time Machine* (full version). 335pp. 5⅜ × 8½. (Available in U.S. only) 20605-X Pa. $5.95

APICIUS COOKERY AND DINING IN IMPERIAL ROME, edited and translated by Joseph Dommers Vehling. Oldest known cookbook in existence offers readers a clear picture of what foods Romans ate, how they prepared them, etc. 49 illustrations. 301pp. 6⅛ × 9¼. 23563-7 Pa. $6.50

SHAKESPEARE LEXICON AND QUOTATION DICTIONARY, Alexander Schmidt. Full definitions, locations, shades of meaning of every word in plays and poems. More than 50,000 exact quotations. 1,485pp. 6½ × 9¼. 22726-X, 22727-8 Pa., Two-vol. set $27.90

THE WORLD'S GREAT SPEECHES, edited by Lewis Copeland and Lawrence W. Lamm. Vast collection of 278 speeches from Greeks to 1970. Powerful and effective models; unique look at history. 842pp. 5⅜ × 8½. 20468-5 Pa. $11.95

THE BLUE FAIRY BOOK, Andrew Lang. The first, most famous collection, with many familiar tales: Little Red Riding Hood, Aladdin and the Wonderful Lamp, Puss in Boots, Sleeping Beauty, Hansel and Gretel, Rumpelstiltskin; 37 in all. 138 illustrations. 390pp. 5⅜ × 8½. 21437-0 Pa. $5.95

THE STORY OF THE CHAMPIONS OF THE ROUND TABLE, Howard Pyle. Sir Launcelot, Sir Tristram and Sir Percival in spirited adventures of love and triumph retold in Pyle's inimitable style. 50 drawings, 31 full-page. xviii + 329pp. 6½ × 9¼. 21883-X Pa. $6.95

AUDUBON AND HIS JOURNALS, Maria Audubon. Unmatched two-volume portrait of the great artist, naturalist and author contains his journals, an excellent biography by his granddaughter, expert annotations by the noted ornithologist, Dr. Elliott Coues, and 37 superb illustrations. Total of 1,200pp. 5⅜ × 8.

Vol. I 25143-8 Pa. $8.95
Vol. II 25144-6 Pa. $8.95

GREAT DINOSAUR HUNTERS AND THEIR DISCOVERIES, Edwin H. Colbert. Fascinating, lavishly illustrated chronicle of dinosaur research, 1820's to 1960. Achievements of Cope, Marsh, Brown, Buckland, Mantell, Huxley, many others. 384pp. 5¼ × 8¼. 24701-5 Pa. $6.95

THE TASTEMAKERS, Russell Lynes. Informal, illustrated social history of American taste 1850's–1950's. First popularized categories Highbrow, Lowbrow, Middlebrow. 129 illustrations. New (1979) afterword. 384pp. 6 × 9.
23993-4 Pa. $6.95

DOUBLE CROSS PURPOSES, Ronald A. Knox. A treasure hunt in the Scottish Highlands, an old map, unidentified corpse, surprise discoveries keep reader guessing in this cleverly intricate tale of financial skullduggery. 2 black-and-white maps. 320pp. 5⅜ × 8½. (Available in U.S. only) 25032-6 Pa. $5.95

AUTHENTIC VICTORIAN DECORATION AND ORNAMENTATION IN FULL COLOR: 46 Plates from "Studies in Design," Christopher Dresser. Superb full-color lithographs reproduced from rare original portfolio of a major Victorian designer. 48pp. 9¼ × 12¼. 25083-0 Pa. $7.95

PRIMITIVE ART, Franz Boas. Remains the best text ever prepared on subject, thoroughly discussing Indian, African, Asian, Australian, and, especially, Northern American primitive art. Over 950 illustrations show ceramics, masks, totem poles, weapons, textiles, paintings, much more. 376pp. 5⅜ × 8. 20025-6 Pa. $6.95

SIDELIGHTS ON RELATIVITY, Albert Einstein. Unabridged republication of two lectures delivered by the great physicist in 1920–21. *Ether and Relativity* and *Geometry and Experience*. Elegant ideas in non-mathematical form, accessible to intelligent layman. vi + 56pp. 5⅜ × 8½. 24511-X Pa. $2.95

THE WIT AND HUMOR OF OSCAR WILDE, edited by Alvin Redman. More than 1,000 ripostes, paradoxes, wisecracks: Work is the curse of the drinking classes, I can resist everything except temptation, etc. 258pp. 5⅜ × 8½. 20602-5 Pa. $4:50

ADVENTURES WITH A MICROSCOPE, Richard Headstrom. 59 adventures with clothing fibers, protozoa, ferns and lichens, roots and leaves, much more. 142 illustrations. 232pp. 5⅜ × 8½. 23471-1 Pa. $3.95

THE ART NOUVEAU STYLE BOOK OF ALPHONSE MUCHA: All 72 Plates from "Documents Decoratifs" in Original Color, Alphonse Mucha. Rare copyright-free design portfolio by high priest of Art Nouveau. Jewelry, wallpaper, stained glass, furniture, figure studies, plant and animal motifs, etc. Only complete one-volume edition. 80pp. 9⅜ × 12¼.   24044-4 Pa. $8.95

ANIMALS: 1,419 COPYRIGHT-FREE ILLUSTRATIONS OF MAMMALS, BIRDS, FISH, INSECTS, ETC., edited by Jim Harter. Clear wood engravings present, in extremely lifelike poses, over 1,000 species of animals. One of the most extensive pictorial sourcebooks of its kind. Captions. Index. 284pp. 9 × 12.
                                                                23766-4 Pa. $9.95

OBELISTS FLY HIGH, C. Daly King. Masterpiece of American detective fiction, long out of print, involves murder on a 1935 transcontinental flight—"a very thrilling story"—NY Times. Unabridged and unaltered republication of the edition published by William Collins Sons & Co. Ltd., London, 1935. 288pp. 5⅜ × 8½. (Available in U.S. only)   25036-9 Pa. $4.95

VICTORIAN AND EDWARDIAN FASHION: A Photographic Survey, Alison Gernsheim. First fashion history completely illustrated by contemporary photographs. Full text plus 235 photos, 1840–1914, in which many celebrities appear. 240pp. 6½ × 9¼.   24205-6 Pa. $6.00

THE ART OF THE FRENCH ILLUSTRATED BOOK, 1700–1914, Gordon N. Ray. Over 630 superb book illustrations by Fragonard, Delacroix, Daumier, Doré, Grandville, Manet, Mucha, Steinlen, Toulouse-Lautrec and many others. Preface. Introduction. 633 halftones. Indices of artists, authors & titles, binders and provenances. Appendices. Bibliography. 608pp. 8⅜ × 11¼.   25086-5 Pa. $24.95

THE WONDERFUL WIZARD OF OZ, L. Frank Baum. Facsimile in full color of America's finest children's classic. 143 illustrations by W. W. Denslow. 267pp. 5⅜ × 8½.   20691-2 Pa. $5.95

FRONTIERS OF MODERN PHYSICS: New Perspectives on Cosmology, Relativity, Black Holes and Extraterrestrial Intelligence, Tony Rothman, et al. For the intelligent layman. Subjects include: cosmological models of the universe; black holes; the neutrino; the search for extraterrestrial intelligence. Introduction. 46 black-and-white illustrations. 192pp. 5⅜ × 8½.   24587-X Pa. $6.95

THE FRIENDLY STARS, Martha Evans Martin & Donald Howard Menzel. Classic text marshalls the stars together in an engaging, non-technical survey, presenting them as sources of beauty in night sky. 23 illustrations. Foreword. 2 star charts. Index. 147pp. 5⅜ × 8½.   21099-5 Pa. $3.50

FADS AND FALLACIES IN THE NAME OF SCIENCE, Martin Gardner. Fair, witty appraisal of cranks, quacks, and quackeries of science and pseudoscience: hollow earth, Velikovsky, orgone energy, Dianetics, flying saucers, Bridey Murphy, food and medical fads, etc. Revised, expanded In the Name of Science. "A very able and even-tempered presentation."—The New Yorker. 363pp. 5⅜ × 8.
                                                                20394-8 Pa. $6.50

ANCIENT EGYPT: ITS CULTURE AND HISTORY, J. E Manchip White. From pre-dynastics through Ptolemies: society, history, political structure, religion, daily life, literature, cultural heritage. 48 plates. 217pp. 5⅜ × 8½.   22548-8 Pa. $4.95

SIR HARRY HOTSPUR OF HUMBLETHWAITE, Anthony Trollope. Incisive, unconventional psychological study of a conflict between a wealthy baronet, his idealistic daughter, and their scapegrace cousin. The 1870 novel in its first inexpensive edition in years. 250pp. 5⅜ × 8½. 24953-0 Pa. $5.95

LASERS AND HOLOGRAPHY, Winston E. Kock. Sound introduction to burgeoning field, expanded (1981) for second edition. Wave patterns, coherence, lasers, diffraction, zone plates, properties of holograms, recent advances. 84 illustrations. 160pp. 5⅜ × 8¼. (Except in United Kingdom) 24041-X Pa. $3.50

INTRODUCTION TO ARTIFICIAL INTELLIGENCE: SECOND, EN-LARGED EDITION, Philip C. Jackson, Jr. Comprehensive survey of artificial intelligence—the study of how machines (computers) can be made to act intelligently. Includes introductory and advanced material. Extensive notes updating the main text. 132 black-and-white illustrations. 512pp. 5⅜ × 8½. 24864-X Pa. $8.95

HISTORY OF INDIAN AND INDONESIAN ART, Ananda K. Coomaraswamy. Over 400 illustrations illuminate classic study of Indian art from earliest Harappa finds to early 20th century. Provides philosophical, religious and social insights. 304pp. 6⅜ × 9⅜. 25005-9 Pa. $8.95

THE GOLEM, Gustav Meyrink. Most famous supernatural novel in modern European literature, set in Ghetto of Old Prague around 1890. Compelling story of mystical experiences, strange transformations, profound terror. 13 black-and-white illustrations. 224pp. 5⅜ × 8½. (Available in U.S. only) 25025-3 Pa. $5.95

ARMADALE, Wilkie Collins. Third great mystery novel by the author of *The Woman in White* and *The Moonstone*. Original magazine version with 40 illustrations. 597pp. 5⅜ × 8½. 23429-0 Pa. $9.95

PICTORIAL ENCYCLOPEDIA OF HISTORIC ARCHITECTURAL PLANS, DETAILS AND ELEMENTS: With 1,880 Line Drawings of Arches, Domes, Doorways, Facades, Gables, Windows, etc., John Theodore Haneman. Sourcebook of inspiration for architects, designers, others. Bibliography. Captions. 141pp. 9 × 12. 24605-1 Pa. $6.95

BENCHLEY LOST AND FOUND, Robert Benchley. Finest humor from early 30's, about pet peeves, child psychologists, post office and others. Mostly unavailable elsewhere. 73 illustrations by Peter Arno and others. 183pp. 5⅜ × 8½. 22410-4 Pa. $3.95

ERTÉ GRAPHICS, Erté. Collection of striking color graphics: *Seasons, Alphabet, Numerals, Aces* and *Precious Stones*. 50 plates, including 4 on covers. 48pp. 9⅜ × 12¼. 23580-7 Pa. $6.95

THE JOURNAL OF HENRY D. THOREAU, edited by Bradford Torrey, F. H. Allen. Complete reprinting of 14 volumes, 1837–61, over two million words; the sourcebooks for *Walden*, etc. Definitive. All original sketches, plus 75 photographs. 1,804pp. 8½ × 12¼. 20312-3, 20313-1 Cloth., Two-vol. set $80.00

CASTLES: THEIR CONSTRUCTION AND HISTORY, Sidney Toy. Traces castle development from ancient roots. Nearly 200 photographs and drawings illustrate moats, keeps, baileys, many other features. Caernarvon, Dover Castles, Hadrian's Wall, Tower of London, dozens more. 256pp. 5⅜ × 8¼. 24898-4 Pa. $5.95

AMERICAN CLIPPER SHIPS: 1833–1858, Octavius T. Howe & Frederick C. Matthews. Fully-illustrated, encyclopedic review of 352 clipper ships from the period of America's greatest maritime supremacy. Introduction. 109 halftones. 5 black-and-white line illustrations. Index. Total of 928pp. 5⅜ × 8½.
25115-2, 25116-0 Pa., Two-vol. set $17.90

TOWARDS A NEW ARCHITECTURE, Le Corbusier. Pioneering manifesto by great architect, near legendary founder of "International School." Technical and aesthetic theories, views on industry, economics, relation of form to function, "mass-production spirit," much more. Profusely illustrated. Unabridged translation of 13th French edition. Introduction by Frederick Etchells. 320pp. 6⅛ × 9¼. (Available in U.S. only)
25023-7 Pa. $8.95

THE BOOK OF KELLS, edited by Blanche Cirker. Inexpensive collection of 32 full-color, full-page plates from the greatest illuminated manuscript of the Middle Ages, painstakingly reproduced from rare facsimile edition. Publisher's Note. Captions. 32pp. 9⅜ × 12¼.
24345-1 Pa. $4.95

BEST SCIENCE FICTION STORIES OF H. G. WELLS, H. G. Wells. Full novel *The Invisible Man,* plus 17 short stories: "The Crystal Egg," "Aepyornis Island," "The Strange Orchid," etc. 303pp. 5⅜ × 8½. (Available in U.S. only)
21531-8 Pa. $4.95

AMERICAN SAILING SHIPS: Their Plans and History, Charles G. Davis. Photos, construction details of schooners, frigates, clippers, other sailcraft of 18th to early 20th centuries—plus entertaining discourse on design, rigging, nautical lore, much more. 137 black-and-white illustrations. 240pp. 6⅛ × 9¼.
24658-2 Pa. $5.95

ENTERTAINING MATHEMATICAL PUZZLES, Martin Gardner. Selection of author's favorite conundrums involving arithmetic, money, speed, etc., with lively commentary. Complete solutions. 112pp. 5⅜ × 8½.
25211-6 Pa. $2.95

THE WILL TO BELIEVE, HUMAN IMMORTALITY, William James. Two books bound together. Effect of irrational on logical, and arguments for human immortality. 402pp. 5⅜ × 8½.
20291-7 Pa. $7.50

THE HAUNTED MONASTERY and THE CHINESE MAZE MURDERS, Robert Van Gulik. 2 full novels by Van Gulik continue adventures of Judge Dee and his companions. An evil Taoist monastery, seemingly supernatural events; overgrown topiary maze that hides strange crimes. Set in 7th-century China. 27 illustrations. 328pp. 5⅜ × 8½.
23502-5 Pa. $5.95

CELEBRATED CASES OF JUDGE DEE (DEE GOONG AN), translated by Robert Van Gulik. Authentic 18th-century Chinese detective novel; Dee and associates solve three interlocked cases. Led to Van Gulik's own stories with same characters. Extensive introduction. 9 illustrations. 237pp. 5⅜ × 8½.
23337-5 Pa. $4.95

Prices subject to change without notice.
Available at your book dealer or write for free catalog to Dept. GI, Dover Publications, Inc., 31 East 2nd St., Mineola, N.Y. 11501. Dover publishes more than 175 books each year on science, elementary and advanced mathematics, biology, music, art, literary history, social sciences and other areas.